How to know

THE UNHINDERED

FLOW

of God's Revelation

to Gloria

Be Still and Know

The Power of the flow.

Harold Herrick Jr.

How to know

The Unhindered

FLOW

of God's Revelation

Harold J. Frelix Sr. & Frances L. Frelix

Pleasant Word
A Division of WINEPRESS PUBLISHING

ISBN 1-4141-0438-3
Library of Congress Catalog Card Number: 2005903342

Ho, every one that thirsteth, come ye to the waters, and he that hath no money; come ye, buy, and eat; yea, come, buy wine and milk without money and without price. Wherefore do ye spend money for that which is not bread? and your labour for that which satisfieth not? hearken diligently unto me, and eat ye that which is good, and let your soul delight itself in fatness. Incline your ear, and come unto me: hear, and your soul shall live; and I will make an everlasting covenant with you, even the sure mercies of David.

—Isa. 55:1-2

For as the rain cometh down, and the snow from heaven, and returneth not thither, but watereth the earth, and maketh it bring forth and bud, that it may give seed to the sower, and bread to the eater: So shall my Word be that goeth forth out of my mouth: it shall not return unto me void, but it shall accomplish that which I please, and it shall prosper in the thing whereto I sent it.

—Isa. 55:10-11

But as it is written, Eye hath not seen, nor ear heard, neither have entered into the heart of man, the things which God hath prepared for them that love him. But God hath revealed them unto us by his Spirit: for the Spirit searcheth all things, yea, the deep things of God. For what man knoweth the things of a man, save the Spirit of man which is in him? even so the things of

God knoweth no man, but the Spirit of God. Now we have received, not the Spirit of the world, but the Spirit which is of God; that we might know the things that are freely given to us of God. Which things also we speak, not in the words which man's wisdom teacheth, but which the Holy Ghost teacheth; comparing spiritual things with spiritual. But the natural man receiveth not the things of the Spirit of God: for they are foolishness unto him: neither can he know them, because they are spiritually discerned.

—1 Cor. 2:9-14

WHAT HINDERS THE FLOW
OF THE HOLY SPIRIT?

WHERE IS THE POWER?

WHERE ARE THE MIRACLES?

WHAT HINDERS THE MANIFESTATION OF
THE HOLY SPIRIT AND THE
CHURCH'S CAPACITY TO USE
THE GIFTS OF THE HOLY SPIRIT?

Table of Contents

PART I

POWER BELONGS TO GOD

The power is in the life of God.

God hath spoken once; twice have I heard this; that power belongeth unto God.

—Ps. 62:11

And this is the record, that God hath given to us eternal life, and this life is in his Son.

—1 John 5:11

He that hath the Son hath life; and he that hath not the Son of God hath not life.

—1 John 5:12

CHAPTER 1

What Happened to the Apostolic Power?

The supernatural birth and growth of the powerful church of Christ is recorded in the book of Acts! By the dynamic, explosive (dunamis) power of the Holy Spirit, the apostles walked with boldness, healing, delivering, advancing God's kingdom, tearing down Satan's kingdom, teaching, evangelizing, turning the whole world upside down!

The church as recorded in the book of Acts is indeed a powerful church. She truly represented the body of Christ, walking in the power of the Holy Spirit as Jesus did.

The church that Christ built is like a mighty rushing river, bringing life to all in its path.

Jesus said in John 14:12, "Verily, verily, I say unto you, He that believeth on me, the works that I do shall he do also; and greater works than these shall he do; *because* I go unto my Father."

So when we look at the book of Acts we see the following evidences of the Spirit: The casting out of unclean spirits, three thousand souls saved in one service, the church praying and God blessing them with great healing power, the cripple healed at the Gate Beautiful that results in praising and praying causing the very earth to quake, and the Holy Spirit speaking through the saints languages that can be understood by foreign peoples. The Holy Spirit seats Himself as a flame upon the heads of the believers. Healings occurred as the apostles' shadows fall on believers. Napkins were sent out with prayers to effect blessings and supernatural healings. Indeed the church moved as a mighty army throughout the land of Israel. And finally we see believers giving themselves and all that they have to the work of the church.

THAT'S POWER. BUT IT'S GOD'S POWER. THERE IS NO OTHER POWER. Power is in God. POWER BELONGS TO GOD. The power is in the life of God.

God hath spoken once; twice have I heard this; that power belongeth unto God.

—Ps. 62:11

And this is the record, that God hath given to us eternal life, and this life is in his Son. He that hath the Son hath life; and he that hath not the Son of God hath not life.

—1 John 5:11-12

In order to have power, we must have God abiding in us and the Word is God.

"In the beginning was the Word and the Word was with God and the Word was God.

—John 1:1

And the Word was made flesh, and dwelt among us, (and we beheld his glory, the glory as of the only begotten of the Father,) full of grace and truth.

—John 1:14

If a man love me, he will keep my words: and my Father will love him, <u>and we will come unto him, and make our abode with him.</u> (Underlining for emphasis)

—John 14:23

If ye abide in me, and my words abide in you, ye shall ask what ye will, and it shall be done unto you.

—John 15:7

We know that Jesus Christ is the same yesterday, today and forever. The Bible tells us that the Lord is immutable, unchangeable, and in Him is no variableness, nor shadow of turning.

Where is the power that the apostles knew? Where are the miracles that the early Christians witnessed? What has caused the change in the church? She is practically unrecognizable compared to the power of the mighty church birthed on the Day of Pentecost.

What has caused her feebleness? She carries the name but the power is not evident.

Instead of the mighty rushing river, today we see that the church has become stagnated, lifeless, and powerless. The mighty flow as related in the book of Acts, of knowledge and power from the Holy Spirit has been stemmed; the flow has ebbed. This book answers the question, "What has hindered the mighty flow of knowledge and power from the Holy Spirit and how can we remove the impediments?"

What has happened to the church? Where is that great power that Peter, James, John, and the apostles walked in? Where are the miracles?

The weakness of the church and our incapacity to see the supernatural both have to do with hindrances to the abundant flow of the Holy Spirit. God's intent for the church is that she walks in power, receiving from Him generously and continuously, but something has blocked the abundant supply.

The primary hindrance has to do with failure to fear God and the failure to believe God's Word. Failure to fear God has to do with the Word of God being lightly treated and therefore, not obeyed.

We know that it's true that the Word of God shall judge us in the last day. Knowing that Jesus, the conquering King, shall return in anger and vengeance in the last day, *referring to Himself as the Word of God,* there ought to be a fear in us and a humility when we approach this almighty Word. For we know that His arm is not shortened, his ear is not filled, nor His eye dimmed. He is as He always was, the active, Almighty, loving, righteous Creator of all things, working according to His own will by His own counsel to serve His own pleasure to the end that His own glory be established in all of reality! He (the Word of God) is not to be taken lightly, but is to be reverenced and obeyed!

Even though *some* miracles are there, we are often incapable of seeing them. We cannot see them because faith must be sight for us. And faith is by the Word of God. Many do not believe the Word of God, have no fear for the Word of God, and have disrespected the Word of God by reason of their carnal minds, actually believing that they have capacity to manipulate the Word Himself. This borders on blasphemy. For the Word, *if* it finds us worthy, will manipulate our tiny minds, renew and restore us to a relationship with our heavenly Father.

When our relationship with the Father is renewed, what great miracles shall be seen, what supernatural gifts may be realized, what revelations shall be received. But first, we must shuffle off this analytical, haughty mind and come to His living Word in humble fear! Wasn't this so with Paul after his conversion? Paul, upon encountering the powerful, living Word, came to fear and reverence of Him. Paul received the abundant flow of revelational knowledge and became a mighty man of God!

It is God's job to give wisdom and our job to be available to receive it. Wisdom comes from the mouth of God, but before wisdom comes humility and before knowledge comes fear. This is the Word of God.

The Bible, the living Word seeks to introduce us to the King of Hearts, Father of Love, the omnipotent, omniscient, eternal, KIND, LOVING, MERCIFUL, GRACIOUS AND GOOD, GOD OUR FATHER.

For the Word of God is quick, and powerful, and sharper than any two edged sword, piercing even to the dividing asunder of soul and Spirit, and of the joints and marrow, and is a discerner of the thoughts and intents of the heart.

—Heb. 4:12

The Word is just as alive and powerful today as He always has been. He is powerful and He knows us. If there is change, it cannot be in Him. Perfection by its very nature cannot become imperfection neither can it become better. Therefore perfection is immutable.

God is our source. There is no failure in the source. The power is still the same. The supply is still available. Whenever the supply seems scarce it is always because there is a blockage. There must be a failure in us. We ourselves have blocked the flow of knowledge and power because we have believed ourselves to be master of the Word instead of allowing the Word to be our master and to master us.

The Word of God is the Spirit of God, is the Son of God, is the mind of Christ and we have not given due regard in our approach to know Him. We have disobeyed the Word which says to us, "Fear God and humble thyself under the mighty hand of God"

The problem must be that we have not really believed that God, by His Word, is revealing to us all needed wisdom and knowledge of Himself and His way and His will. Because we do not fear Him, we have become haphazard in our approach unto His living Word, which is Himself. Because of this we seek to approach

Him in the haughtiness of our human mental capacity and not with an attitude of patiently waiting in faith for His revelation.

God resists the proud and gives grace to the humble *(James 4:6)*. If we would desire to serve Him and be called according to His purpose, if we would humble ourselves under His mighty hand then God will exalt us in due time; He will manifest Himself in us.

Yes, we have caused Him to resist us because of our haughty pride. Therefore, some, though they be saints are not getting the full flow of wisdom and knowledge from God that only the fearful and the humble are receiving.

What do we think we are doing when we approach the Word of God? To approach His Word is to approach Himself. Academically we (humanity) approach Him (His Word) with the attitude that by sheer concentration of mind in analytical dissection we can reduce the Word to its simplest form and consume it in finite-sized pieces and by so doing, comprehend God. In other words, we really have the idea that we are able to break the Word down. What an insult to almighty God! What high-stepping humanity! It is no wonder that God resists our intellectual pursuits and high-mindedness and gives His revelation to the lowly and to those who approach with a genuine attitude of awesome respect as did the apostles.

Now let's look again at the book of Acts, the apostles walking in great power! They were walking in the will of God, in one accord, fearful, and great grace was upon them all. Now that's unlimited power!

And being let go, they went to their own company, and reported all that the chief priests and elders had said unto them.

And when they heard that, they lifted up their voice to God with one accord, and said, Lord, thou art God, which hast made heaven, and earth, and the sea, and all that in them is:

Who by the mouth of thy servant David hast said, Why did the heathen rage, and the people imagine vain things? The kings of the earth stood up, and the rulers were gathered together against the Lord, and against his Christ. For of a truth against thy holy child Jesus, whom thou hast anointed, both Herod, and Pontius Pilate, with the Gentiles, and the people of Israel, were gathered together, For to do whatsoever thy hand and thy counsel determined before to be done. And now, Lord, behold their threatenings: and grant unto thy servants, that with all boldness they may speak thy Word, By stretching forth thine hand to heal; and that signs and wonders may be done by the name of thy holy child Jesus. And when they had prayed, the place was shaken where they were assembled together; and they were all filled with the Holy Ghost, and they spake the Word of God with boldness. And the multitude of them that believed were of one heart and of one soul: neither said any of them that ought of the things which he possessed was his own; but they had all things common. And with great power gave the apostles witness of the resurrection of the Lord Jesus: and great grace was upon them all.

—Acts 4:23–33

What Happened to the Apostolic Power?

And great fear came upon all the church, and upon as many as heard these things. And by the hands of the apostles were many signs and wonders wrought among the people; (and they were all with one accord in Solomon's porch.

And of the rest durst no man join himself to them: but the people magnified them.

And believers were the more added to the Lord, multitudes both of men and women.)

Insomuch that they brought forth the sick into the streets, and laid them on beds and couches, that at the least the shadow of Peter passing by might overshadow some of them. There came also a multitude out of the cities round about unto Jerusalem, bringing sick folks, and them which were vexed with unclean spirits: and they were healed every one.

—Acts 5:11–16

And God wrought special miracles by the hands of Paul:

So that from his body were brought unto the sick handkerchiefs or aprons, and the diseases departed from them, and the evil spirits went out of them.

Then certain of the vagabond Jews, exorcists, took upon them to call over them which had evil Spirits the name of the Lord Jesus, saying, We adjure you by Jesus whom Paul preacheth. And there were seven sons of one Sceva, a Jew, and chief of the priests, which did so. And the evil Spirit answered and said, Jesus I know, and Paul I know; but who are ye? And the man in whom the evil spirit was leaped on them, and overcame them, and prevailed against them, so that they fled out of that house naked and wounded.

And this was known to all the Jews and Greeks also dwelling at Ephesus; and fear fell on them all, and the name of the Lord Jesus was magnified. And many that believed came, and confessed, and showed their deeds. Many of them also which used curious arts brought their books together, and burned them before all men: and they counted the price of them, and found it fifty thousand pieces of silver. So mightily grew the Word of God and prevailed.

—Acts 19:11–20

That is who the true church is! That is who the body of Christ is! The church today also has the capacity to walk in the power of God. We have been endued with the same Holy Spirit; God's Word has not changed; Jesus Christ, the head has not changed. Something has happened that has caused the body of Christ to be weakened. We ourselves have limited the reception of power from God!

CHAPTER 2

Jesus Said Upon This Rock I Will Build My Church

Peter received revelation from God that Jesus was the Christ, the Son of the living God. Only the Father can reveal the Son.

> *And Jesus answered and said unto him, Blessed art thou, Simon Barjona: for flesh and blood hath not revealed it unto thee, but my Father which is in heaven. And I say also unto thee, That thou art Peter, and "upon this rock I will build my church;" and the gates of hell shall not prevail against it.*
>
> —Matt. 16:17

This is how the church is built. It is built upon the Father revealing the Son. This is the rock of knowledge upon which the church is built, knowledge revealed by the Father of the Son.

Each soul who has received revelation from the Father that Jesus Christ is the Son of God and believes on Him is born again. The church, the called out ones, the Word-beings, are no longer human beings, but supernaturally born of the powerful Word of God!

We know that the Word of God is quick, and powerful and sharper than any two-edged sword. Therefore, we must be born of the Word. This is where our power resides. Our power resides in the Word of God.

The church cannot be powerful; indeed, the church cannot be church except it be born of the Word. That which is born of the Word is Spirit. The church becomes spiritual by birth and that not of itself; it is the work of the Word in reproduction. Every person knows that no one arranges his own birth, but is passive and unformed until the power of life is generated to it by the will of that which is life.

Upon our new birth we become Word-babies, born of the Word. Word-babies are nurtured and empowered by the Word of God. The Word, when received, grows in us.

> *But he answered and said, It is written, Man shall not live by bread alone, but by every Word that proceedeth out of the mouth of God.*
> —John 6:35

> *And Jesus said unto them, I am the bread of life: he that cometh to me shall never hunger; and he that believeth on me shall never thirst.*
> —Matt. 4:4

At that time Jesus answered and said, I thank thee, O Father, Lord of heaven and earth, because thou hast hid these things from the wise and prudent, and hast revealed them unto babes.

—Matt. 11:25

God gives power to his children, his little ones, who make themselves intentionally available, humbling themselves to receive His Word in revelation.

God hath spoken once; twice have I heard this; that power belongeth unto God.

—Ps. 62:11

The church is to submit herself to the Word of God, Christ the King. When she submits herself to the Word, she is empowered to fulfill her purpose.

The church has been empowered as the body of Christ to preach the gospel to the poor, heal the brokenhearted, preach deliverance to the captives and the recovering of sight to the blind, to set at liberty them that are bruised, and to preach the acceptable year of the Lord.

We say this because Jesus said in John 20:21, "…. *Peace be unto you: as my Father hath sent me, even so send I you.*" The church is the body of Christ and is therefore to operate as the Word of God sent forth into all the world to accomplish the will of the Father. As He is, so are we in the world.

God has work for the church to do! The church is the agent of the Word of God going forth in power! God has commissioned the church to preach and teach.

The whole intent of the church is to obey, honor, and glorify the Father by the power of Christ in us. The preaching of the gospel is the work of the church. The church by its preaching is to deliver, to heal, to give sight, and to free those to whom it is sent (*Luke 4:18*). The Word of God in the church will not return to God except it fulfill His will and accomplish that whereunto He sent it. *The Word accomplishes and will not return to God until it is finished!*

The Gates of Hell Shall Not Prevail Against the Church

What are the gates of hell? The gates of hell are the rebellious lies and all that is born out of it. This is that rebellion that has put humanity in the bonds of sin, hell, and death, and held all men in darkness and disobedience. The gates of hell hold humanity captive and attempts to set up blocks to prevent the truth, which is the Word of God, from entering into the heart of man. The gates of hell attempt to block the light of the Word so that the soul remains in darkness. Revelation of the Word of God is the only way that Satan, the deceiver, is defeated. The Revelation of the Word tears down the gates of hell.

God must give us knowledge as to what weapon to use against Satan's lies, when to use it and how. We are not capable of coming against the gates of hell except we have revelation as to its structure, and knowledge of the proper weapon or weapons that we are to use in its defeat. The lie keeps us bound, even though it is only an illusion. Its power is confusion, darkness, fear and chaos. If Satan can keep us confused, fearful, or in darkness he can keep us in bondage. If we receive the Word, the truth exposes the lie and makes us free. We cannot come against the lie except we have sheer power and knowledge in the Word of God.

> *For though we walk in the flesh, we do not war after the flesh: (For the weapons of our warfare are not carnal, but mighty through God to the pulling down of strong holds;) Casting down imaginations, and every high thing that exalteth itself against the knowledge of God, and bringing into captivity every thought to the obedience of Christ; And having in a readiness to revenge all disobedience, when your obedience is fulfilled.*
> —2 Cor. 10:3-6

Our warfare is against the gates of hell and we are empowered to overcome the gates. The gates of hell exalts itself against the knowledge of God. We are empowered and overcome by the Holy Spirit within us. Each saint is endowed with the life and presence of God, which is sheer power. It is a strange thing, but God has endued us with power to be witnesses unto Him and to speak the truth in love.

Why Are The Gates of Hell Prevailing?

Why do we see so many still imprisoned by the lies of Satan? The church is weak and many perish for the lack of knowledge. God has made his knowledge readily available, but man in his pride does not seek to receive God's knowledge in meekness but by his brute capacity to obtain. In other words, man seeks God's knowledge by his own capacity to discover it. Man does not allow God's almighty and powerful Word to manipulate him. Our carnality does not allow God to secrete knowledge into the new self to which God gives birth. Therefore, the saint's growth is stunted because the flow of revelational knowledge is ebbed. The saint therefore does not receive what it needs for growth and strengthening.

> *Go ye therefore, and teach all nations, baptizing them in the name of the Father, and of the Son, and of the Holy Ghost.*
>
> —Matt. 28:18

> *And he said unto them, Go ye into all the world, and preach the gospel to every creature. He that believeth and is baptized shall be saved; but he that believeth not shall be damned. And these signs shall follow them that believe; In my name shall they cast out devils; they shall speak with new tongues; They shall take up serpents; and if they drink any deadly thing, it shall not hurt them; they shall lay hands on the sick, and they shall recover.*
>
> —Mark 16:15

Behold, I give unto you power to tread on serpents and scorpions, and over all the power of the enemy: and nothing shall by any means hurt you.

—Luke 10:19

Jesus Christ, the head, is holding out to the body of Christ the knowledge and wisdom it needs to overcome all that opposes her as she seeks to deliver souls from the gates of hell that they might come to Christ. Yet the body of Christ deteriorates because it seeks to aggressively and willfully obtain rather than to humbly receive.

When we look and see the powerful gates of hell all around us, when we see the darkness, the hopeless faces of the captives, the walking dead, the confused, the oppressed, the question is, where is this church that Christ has built? We see groups that carry the name of "church" on every corner, but where is this church that Christ was referring to when he said, "Upon this rock I will build my church and the gates of hell shall not prevail against it"?

The church stands, the gates of hell are before her, but the church is hindered for lack of knowledge and therefore lack of power. The church has not trusted and therefore has not received what Christ willingly desires to give them. Christ truly desires for the church to walk in apostolic power in order to be effective in the gathering process. Christ's desire is that the church be so powerful that hell's gates would fall at her presence.

What is it that is stemming this flow of knowledge and power that comes from the Holy Spirit? Again, is it not pride that instigates human imagination to be lifted up against the knowledge of God? Whereby we have undertaken by force of our intelligence to find out the things of God, to decode His sacred Word. We in high-mindedness have believed that we could attain to the knowledge by coercion of what we have supposed to be the sleeping Word that awaits our press for information. The Word is not asleep; the Word is alive and powerful, and gushing forth. However, there are limited numbers of vessels in position to receive!

> *For what man knoweth the things of a man, save the spirit of man which is in him? even so the things of God knoweth no man, but the Spirit of God. Now we have received, not the spirit of the world, but the Spirit which is of God; that we might know the things that are freely given to us of God.*
>
> —1 Cor. 2:11

There is an abundance of knowledge, flowing down from the mouth of God, like a free-flowing fountain; however, the flow is blocked, preventing the vessels from being filled. There is no lack in the source, only the vessels. The Word is able to do its work. God promised us that His Word would not return void but that it would accomplish what He sent it down to do. God wants some things done in the people for whom His Son died, for those who have believed on Him. God has work for the Word to do in us.

God empowers those of us who will humbly sit in faith before the Word and allow the Word to speak to our spirit selves giving us wisdom. Then when the time comes that God sends someone our way or puts someone in our path who is in darkness and without hope, out of our bellies shall flow rivers of living water. If that person is receptive and open, the Word that we give will bring life to that person, releasing him from Satan's clutches. This doesn't happen because we are smart but because the Lord has prepared us for that hour. We must be willing to be used of God to speak things spiritually, asking Him to give us wisdom that out of us shall flow rivers of living water. So we must make ourselves available in faith and thereby receive. Then we can pray, "Lord, use me." When we open our mouths in faith we will see God operate our Spirit and speak to a person at a level that our carnal mind cannot reach.

That's how people are saved—it's a spiritual thing, it's a Holy Ghost thing, it's a partnership thing. If we will submit and make ourselves available, God will use us.

Whatever word God gives us to give to someone, we must faithfully give. We've got to trust God to be God. What if we give someone the gospel and they storm out angry? God's Word is alive, He is powerful, and He knows all things; trust Him! Don't become doubtful, don't back up, and don't get scared. The Lord has prepared us for this hour; this person is important to the Lord, Jesus said in John 12:27, *"Now is my soul troubled; and what shall I say? Father, save me from this hour: but for this cause came I unto this hour."* So we must remove ourselves out of the equation and simply be the vessels and not the source. Because we received the revelation from God, we put down our intelligence, our degree, our street smarts long enough for God to use us then we are able to be used by God. There will be those who reject God's Word but God in His love has faithfully used His vessels (that's us) to speak His Word in love. There will be those that will receive the Word and not reject it. We have given them what they needed. This is how we tear down the gates of hell!

The church must submit herself humbly under the living Word of God that she might maintain life and bring forth life unto her husband, Jesus Christ. We are saying that the proper approach to the *Word is humble submission and faith that the Word is able.* We are also saying that the ability the Word has is that it can inform us and guide us and create in us the new creature according to God's holy will. We are saying that this is not due to human effort or human will but that the active Word of God that is alive, quickens us if we will make ourselves humbly available to it and let our brain activity be still.

Water from a pitcher can only be poured into a glass or vessel if the vessel is positioned lower than the pitcher. The water flows downward. This is how a saint receives revelation from God, not in high-mindedness, but waiting humbly before Him to receive His unhindered flow.

> *And there are three that bear witness in earth, the Spirit, and the water, and the blood: and these three agree in one.*
>
> —1 John 5:8

According to 1 John 5:7-8, the water, the blood and the Spirit are in behavioral agreement. They all characteristically have a downward flow. Humility therefore is *the necessity* for an uninterrupted flow of Holy Spirit communication

> *In that hour Jesus rejoiced in Spirit, and said, I thank thee, O Father, Lord of heaven and earth, that thou hast hid these things from the wise and prudent, and hast revealed them unto babes: even so, Father; for so it seemed good in thy sight.*
>
> —Luke 10:21

God resists those who would approach Him with a high mind. We cannot emphasize this enough. It is therefore that we submit to you that we, even the children of God, must approach Him with all humility and lowliness of mind, seeking His grace as children waiting for the parent's instructions. We call this *making ourselves available to receive revelational knowledge from the Word of God.* This is a humble thing.

Revelational Knowledge, the Only Real Knowledge

Why are we talking about revelational knowledge? Because the only real knowledge of God is revelational knowledge. We did not come to it by virtue of our strong humanly informed minds, but by the grace of God as He shows to us the things we need to know from the Spirit realm. God teaches us how to walk in the light of His knowledge.

The difference between revelational knowledge and what the world's system calls knowledge is the goal. The world's goal is to gratify the flesh with egoist and temporal things. The world wants to say, "I have accomplished the knowledge of God." God's goal for His humble ones is that they be still and know that He is God and that all knowledge is given to the humble who make themselves available.

Revelational knowledge is that abiding content of understanding which is granted to the Spirit-man by the living, powerful Word of God. That Word of God is a person and a written proposition of Holy Scripture. It is one. It is unified. It is identical in power to represent the Father.

The Word is the Father's perfect expression; however, the Word has expressed the everlasting Father in the creation of heaven and earth. Not that these things are exhaustive depictions or descriptions, but they are true.

Only truth can rightly be called knowledge. And truth, because of its superlative nature and content and because it must exist without fallibility, is the revelation of God. Truth has such perfection that God identifies Himself as Truth. When we have received of the truth we have received of the nature of God Himself. For that reason we understand the Word that Christ gave us when He said, "My Word shall never pass away." The Word is Spirit; the Word is truth; the truth is God. *Hallelujah!*

Humanity has never been able to find truth out, because ultimately truth is God and God is truth.

He made known his ways unto Moses, his acts unto the children of Israel.

—Ps. 103:7

Man cannot find out God and he cannot know the way of God unless God makes it known unto him. Therefore it is by revelation. Residual content of truth in a being must be retained in the spiritual aspect of the being for truth is spiritual and does not reside in matter, but material being inferior and finite, must abide in the Spirit. The spiritual is neither finite nor limited by things finite.

My flesh abides in my Spirit self, but my flesh is not big enough to contain my Spirit self.

In other words, I must receive the Word of God into my Spirit, for the Word is Spirit and the Word is truth. It is not head knowledge but spiritual knowledge, revealed knowledge. It is superior to the flesh and the fleshly mind. Flesh cannot hold the truth; the Spirit receives it. In my flesh dwelleth no good thing!

Only that which is permanent and eternal is true. And that which is not permanent and is subject to destruction or cessation is not real to the extent that it is temporal. It also, therefore, could not be identified with truth. Truth is not temporal; it's perfect and eternal. So false spirit and true Spirit exists right now because of time, but when time ceases and eternity—past, present and future—are one there will be no more lies and no more rebellion. That which is imperfect shall pass away. God will have put everything under the Son. God alone shall be exalted in that day. *Thank you, Jesus!*

Whose voice then shook the earth: but now he hath promised, saying, Yet once more I shake not the earth only, but also heaven. And this Word, Yet once more, signifieth the removing of those things that are shaken, as of things that are made, that those things which cannot be shaken may remain.

—Matthew 24:35

Heaven and earth shall pass away, but my words shall not pass away.

—Heb. 13:26-27

Here in our Revelational Knowledge Institute we are putting forth knowledge that is revealed. We are sure that it is knowledge due to its source and effect. Its source is God; its effect is eternal life. It is therefore we are saying that we are putting forth revelational knowledge. We did not attain to it, we did not construe, construct or otherwise cause it, but we subjected ourselves and believed and God has been faithful. We received God's truth to the setting aside of the knowledge that we thought we had. We have content that is not comprehended by the darkness that we are, nor modified by the lie we have known. That content is knowledge—not just knowledge however, but true knowledge, holy and eternal.

For us, knowledge is defined as the internal treasury of eternal truth. Whatsoever therefore is not eternal is lie and is not knowledge. So all of the content that is labeled as knowledge may not be so. Finite mind cannot define knowledge. One must be infinite in order to call knowledge knowledge, for if he is finite he cannot stretch wide enough, high enough, or deep enough to test content of reality. Therefore God is the only one who can designate truth and knowledge as such. It is He with whom we have to do. Only God is capable of revealing God. That which is less than God can be true but not truth.

His eyes were as a flame of fire, and on his head were many crowns; and he had a name written, that no man knew, but he himself.

—Rev. 19:12

He had a name written that no man knew but He Himself and to whomever He would reveal it. The name is the Word of God. He is truth and the residual of His revelation to the spirit is knowledge.

For there are certain men crept in unawares, who were before of old ordained to this condemnation, ungodly men, turning the grace of our God into lasciviousness, and denying the only Lord God, and our Lord Jesus Christ.

—Jude 1:4

But these speak evil of those things which they know not: but what they know naturally, as brute beasts, in those things they corrupt themselves.

—Jude 1:10

These men that Jude refers to attempt to define the Word of God and say what it is and what it isn't.

And as brute beasts they are fleshly and know nothing of the Word of God. Neither can they be still and be subject and let the Word reveal for there is no place in them for knowledge that comes by revelation. They are not Spirit born but they are natural brute beasts and as such they cannot know things that are spiritually discerned; therefore they are foolish to say that the Word of God is conflicting and that it has fallibility. How could they know?

Things that they know, being brute beasts—such as males are made for females, and vice versa—even this simple knowledge they could not keep, but they have turned it backwards and corrupted themselves.

If you will get a hold of God's Word, God's Word will get a hold of you. You must humble yourself before the Word of God. We must approach the Word of God with humility and be subject to the Word in order to receive from the Word. If not, the Word of God will humble us, because it is greater. Did this not happen as Jacob wrestled with the angel? Attempting to overpower the angel in order to receive a blessing, it was only after he was rendered helpless by the touch of the angel that Jacob was actually in a position to receive.

We must say, I'm going to get the Word in me and let it happen to me. Revelation is spiritual.

There is a universal offering that one would get if he believes the Word of God. He will still get blessed, but he gets in part that which is perfectly offered by God. *When that which is perfect is come....*

The perfect Word speaks to us; however, we only receive in part when we try to pull out of the Word and manipulate the Word. We miss something, we lose something. The Word should be handled with care and concern instead of being brutish.

Jude talks about us being like brute beasts interfering with things that we have no business in. People don't honor holiness, the sweetness of it; we try to pull something apart and dissect it.

The Word known is capable of teaching the Word. If you know the Word, the Word is capable of teaching you the Word. If I know certain things about you I will know what's necessary to know about you even though I don't know all about you. If you are the supply and I have need, if I know you then I can know what I need from you. This Word is so much the truth that if you could take any of it and know it you would not have to know the rest of it. It's alive and true, the global truth of the Word. If I only know so much of it then each time you speak to me, I'll know whether its right or wrong. If you have enough truth to know it the Word will teach you the rest of it. One part defines the rest of it.

> *For the word of God is quick, and powerful, and sharper than any two edged sword, piercing even to the dividing asunder of soul and Spirit, and of the joints and marrow, and is a discerner of the thoughts and intents of the heart.*
>
> —Heb. 4:12

Knowledge will come by revelation if it is actual truth. Knowledge from the Holy Ghost that resides in the spirit is true knowledge. Source has everything to do with whether knowledge is knowledge.

There is no respect for the Holy Spirit; there is no respect for God. We attempt to learn the things of God. Learning has something to do with my own will and capacity. To learn the Word entails the exertion of my active will. This being true I would have something to boast of and this being true the Word would be more available to those who have the greatest mental acuity. Faith would not be the greater factor but intelligence.

THE FAR WEIGHTIER THINGS

Spiritual discernment is a gift received.

For who maketh thee to differ from another? and what hast thou that thou didst not receive? now if thou didst receive it, why dost thou glory, as if thou hadst not received it?

—1 Cor. 4:7

Please understand that we are not seeking earthly knowledge, nor are we seeking to use God's Word to operate in the world order, but we seek God Himself in salvation, obedience and love, to worship Him and to praise Him. We seek Him as spiritual beings that we may walk above the world, not academically as earth dwellers but spiritually, as supernatural Word-beings.

Of course, we believe that television repairmen should go to the electrical video institutes to learn their trade and not to the Bible. We also believe that the plumber should go to plumbing school, the doctors should go to medical school, the lawyers should go to law school to learn their trade. If you are a preacher or a spiritual leader or teacher or a church worker of any kind, then you must realize that the carnal mind is not the issue, but the heavier and more weighty things of life must be revealed to you by the Word of God. Render unto Caesar the things that are Caesar's and render unto God the things that are God's, but you cannot know the things of God except by revelation.

So there is knowledge for carnal life that is useful and there is knowledge for spiritual life from the Father of spirits. We are taught by the Word of God not to love carnal things of this world, only to use them, not to abuse them and not to be used *by* them.

THE SPIRITUAL THINGS OF GOD

But as it is written, Eye hath not seen, nor ear heard, neither have entered into the heart of man, the things which God hath prepared for them that love him. But God hath revealed them unto us by his Spirit: for the Spirit searcheth all things, yea, the deep things of God. For what man knoweth the things of a man, save the Spirit of man which is in him? even so the things of God knoweth no man, but the spirit of God. Now we have received, not the Spirit of the world, but the Spirit which is of God; that we might know the things that are freely given to us of God. Which things also we speak, not in the words which man's wisdom teacheth, but which the Holy Ghost teacheth; comparing spiritual things with spiritual. But the natural man receiveth not

the things of the Spirit of God: for they are foolishness
unto him: neither can he know them, because they are
spiritually discerned.

—1 Cor. 2:9-14

This is the basis or golden text of everything that we are saying here.

We have various intelligent gathering agencies given to us by God so that we are able to abide in a physical world. It allows us to maintain our safety, gain our food, live in a social community and maintain our general physical well being. This agency is called our brain. Its gathering factors are our eyes, ears, nose, along with tactile and taste capabilities. These are the windows by which our brain is able to assess the physical realm and from it gain our necessary life in this reality. But the Bible tells us that eye has not seen neither ear heard, neither has it entered into the heart of man the things that God has prepared for them that love Him.

NOTE…. The scripture above, 1 Corinthians 2 verse 9 does not say us who love Him, but *them* because the person who still knows reality by his intelligent gathering agency has not yet received the spiritual agency of God. And we see that the scripture says that God revealed them to us by His Spirit. This is not a human spirit, it is not a spirit that is in any sense alienated from the Spirit of God, but it is His own essence that one must have in order to receive God's revelation.

In verse 12 above, the scripture says, "..*now we have received not the spirit of the world but the Spirit which is of God that we might know the things that are freely given to us of God, which things also we speak (preach) not in the words which man's wisdom teacheth but which the Holy Ghost teacheth. Comparing spiritual with spiritual."*

> *"...But the natural man receiveth not the things of the Spirit of God for they are foolishness unto him, neither can he know them because they are spiritually discerned."*

—Verse 14

So there is knowledge for carnal life that is good and there is true knowledge for spiritual life from the Father of Spirits, which is superior.

And we can learn and we can obtain and achieve and discover through our natural faculties, brain, eyes, and senses, and obtain knowledge for carnal life but the things of God, as it is written, are spiritually discerned.

Knowledge of this world's system

Learn what you need to learn in order to live in this world. But it is a far *weightier thing* to know God, to know how to serve Him and love Him, and glorify Him. Therefore, we put this above all other priorities of knowledge, that our lives may have ultimate meaning in that we please Him, knowing that this world is not our home.

God has commissioned the church to teach. The Word will enter in and do the work with the teacher and also to those who are taught.

As a lower priority, let us be educated according to the need that we have in this world, that we might be able to function, earn a living and bless our houses and God's house according to His holy will. We must be sure that we are not lovers of this system or of our lives in it. Let us rather set our affections on high that we offend not nor become lost in this present world. For we have a God to glorify and a hell to shun.

WHAT KNOWLEDGE IS NOT!

If you will bear with us in this chapter, we *must* make it very clear *what true knowledge is not!*

As we have previously stated, knowledge is defined as the treasury of internal truth, and whatever is not truth is lie and not knowledge, even if it is labeled knowledge.

Man has set forth many things that they call knowledge which in actuality exalts itself against the knowledge of God.

Man has also attempted to dilute the Word of God. To mix the thoughts of God and man is to reduce perfection to imperfection. It will not make imperfection better, but it will certainly make perfection imperfect.

We must approach God with a pure heart, not mixing in psychology, sociology, human philosophy, etc.

The true meaning of science means knowledge. If it's true knowledge then it's spiritual. Science means knowledge. Knowledge, however, that is carnally appropriated is only as sound as its source. (We know that the carnal mind is extremely fallible according to Romans 8:7 *"Because the carnal mind is enmity against*

God: for it is not subject to the law of God, neither indeed can be.")

> *O Timothy, keep that which is committed to thy trust, avoiding profane and vain babblings, and oppositions of science falsely so called: Which some professing have erred concerning the faith. Grace be with thee. Amen.*
> —1 Tim. 6:20-21

True knowledge is *not* to be found by looking at this world.

True knowledge is not all the heavy psychology, logic, humanistic mindset, evolution, or sociology. True knowledge is not human customs and traditions, nor is it human opinions or superstitions.

> *Are ye so foolish? having begun in the Spirit, are ye now made perfect by the flesh? But now, after that ye have known God, or rather are known of God, how turn ye again to the weak and beggarly elements, whereunto ye desire again to be in bondage?*
> —Gal. 3:3

How can we, after having known God, go back to such foolishness? Let no man spoil you through vain philosophy.

> *Beware lest any man spoil you through philosophy and vain deceit, after the tradition of men, after the rudiments of the world, and not after Christ. For in him dwelleth all the fulness of the Godhead bodily.*
> —Col. 2:8-9

Don't be deceived by the human understanding and empty delusions that man gives after the principles of the world, which is the educational system of the world.

For we have not followed cunningly devised fables, when we made known unto you the power and coming of our Lord Jesus Christ, but were eyewitnesses of his majesty.

—2 Pet. 1:16

For false Christs and false prophets shall rise, and shall show signs and wonders, to seduce, if it were possible, even the elect.

—Mark 14:22

Having these scriptures abiding in us it would seem impossible for the church to be begging humanism for godly knowledge. Even so it seems that the church has done and is doing exactly that, therefore diluting the Word of God and restricting the flow of revelational knowledge.

Sociology is not knowledge. Sociology is man's study of interactions and dynamics between members of society. God has already set forth the truth of human interaction in His Word and we have every model needed for truth.

Human philosophy is not knowledge and is falsely called wisdom.

I thank my God always on your behalf, for the grace of God which is given you by Jesus Christ; That in every thing ye are enriched by him, in all utterance, and in all knowledge; Even as the testimony of Christ was confirmed in you: So that ye come behind in no gift; waiting for the coming of our Lord Jesus Christ:

—1 Cor. 1:4-7

For Christ sent me not to baptize, but to preach the gospel: not with wisdom of Words, lest the cross of Christ should be made of none effect. For the preaching of the cross is to them that perish foolishness; but unto us which are saved it is the power of God. For it is written, I will destroy the wisdom of the wise, and will bring to nothing the understanding of the prudent. Where is the wise? where is the scribe? where is the disputer of this world? hath not God made foolish the wisdom of this world? For after that in the wisdom of God the world by wisdom knew not God, it pleased God by the foolishness of preaching to save them that believe. For the Jews require a sign, and the Greeks seek after wisdom: But we preach Christ crucified, unto the Jews a stumblingblock, and unto the Greeks foolishness; But unto them which are called, both Jews and Greeks, Christ the power of God, and the wisdom of God. Because the foolishness of God is wiser than men; and the weakness of God is stronger than men. For ye see your calling, brethren, how that not many wise men after the flesh, not many mighty, not many noble, are called: But God hath chosen the foolish things of the world to confound the wise; and God hath chosen the weak things of the world to confound the things which are mighty; And base things of the world, and things which are despised, hath God chosen, yea, and things which are not, to bring to nought things that are: That no flesh should glory in his presence. But of him are ye in Christ Jesus, who of God is made unto us wisdom, and righteousness, and sanctification, and redemption: That, according as it is written, He that glorieth, let him glory in the Lord.

—1 Cor. 1:17-31

Any attempted rendering of truth necessarily brings that rendering back to the realm of faith unless it admits to some supernatural presuppositions regarding onto-logical reality. Without faith there must be a reasonable and logical step-by-step explanation for the origin of ma-terial substance. There are also questions of design and purpose which cannot be intellectually or logically dealt with. If a reasonable, purposeful or teleological sound reality is set forth there is an automatic assumption for God. Therefore, the idea or the concept of philosophy in and of itself is begging the question.

We are not setting forth a postulate for an absurd reality for that would be as silly as human science and the big bang. It would be as self-contradictory as a belief that a real and scientific psychology can exist.

Psychology is not knowledge

This godless religion of manifold human theories and haphazard hypothesis is the finest surmising and the most groundless hopes of humanity in its endeavor to realize a reasonable dimension with God. The desire of psychology is to supplant God in the right to decide what is best for man.

It is the natural outgrowth of Adam's decision to eat from the tree of knowledge and be as gods and construct a fluid relative morality. Psychology has as its impetus and drive a thinly-veiled hatred for Jesus Christ. This hatred comes from the liar himself and his hate is the hate of his children, hating God, the saints, and anything that is called God. The father of psychology himself, Sigmund Freud, was an open hater of God. What place has lie with truth?

There is a necessary marriage between psychology and evolution. They hold in common a mutual groundwork of verbosity, lie, and slickness. What they cannot establish in half-truths, they seek to accomplish by dazzling word play. Though they both have failed to be science according to how science is defined, yet they both admire and use one another for foundation. The limit of their speculation is their mind and necessarily having to admit to frailty and incompetence, they each bolster the other and report that of a truth the other is indeed good science.

Evolution is not knowledge

Evolution is the sad attempt to come to accept a reasonable purposeful reality that exists by accident. The purpose of the intent is, of course, to bypass the need for God and establish a universe, as it is, beautiful in its perfect design, good in its manifestation of love, and reasoned within the designated space of humanity. There may be and doubtlessly is, beyond the space of man, that which is beyond reason, but we see a well-reasoned universe that we can understand insofar as our limits are concerned. The idea of evolution however would call for an absurd universe happening by accident without rhyme or reason, just a matter of time and elements *(the big bang theory).* Of course evolution runs into its problem when it seeks to account for elements or material or any such thing in its origin of reality. Dialectical materialism posits that out of conflict and chaos, out of self-seeking and pain avoidance evolves a new being. Dialectical materialism says when an entity mates with another entity and a being battles with another being for survival that by its mating and its battle, a new being emerges which itself undertakes to mate and to battle with other new beings, and so the survival of the fittest species and the cessation of the weaker species, brings forth the higher forms. This is not merely a material effect, but it has become the thought processes of psychology in understanding the place of humanity in the universe. That man thinks in the same terms—thesis, antithesis and synthesis—surrounds us in the teaching that conditions our perceptions of reality. This is what is taught to our children in the school system and is one of the reasons prayer has been so easily removed from the schools. To pray to God would be in direct conflict with the theory that all things consist of themselves by time and chance.

Not a cleverly devised fable

> *For we have not followed cunningly devised fables, when we made known unto you the power and coming of our Lord Jesus Christ, but were eyewitnesses of his majesty.*
>
> —2 Pet. 1:16

True knowledge is not a demonically inspired religion or a cleverly devised fable and did not come out of being too long in one position (lotus) or in seizures in a darkened cave.

Epistemology is not knowledge

Epistemology is the study of knowledge; the study of what philosophers are saying. In other words it is presupposition of psychological learning. This, of course, is not true knowledge in that the source is not truth.

True Knowledge is not learned

There are various types of learning but they do not bring you to true knowledge. Learning is the exercise of reason and response to the environment. There are various levels of learning.

True Knowledge is not academics

Academia involves the things that have been tested and tried and found through the honesty of competent witnesses over the eons of testing to be true.

Academic excellence is no evidence that one has any greater capacity in reception of the revealing Word of God. There is no evidence that receiving all A's in an academic setting of theological endeavor can bring one to leadership capacity in the body of Christ. In fact it seems readily apparent that only by faithful reception of the living Word of God, can that Word have access to an open heart to great revelational knowledge.

Man thinks that if he can look at this Word and just work on it until he comes to some truth, it's as if his mind is working or subjecting something to itself, which is assuming that his mind is superior to the Word.

The truth is, we believe that we must be subject to the Word. We are limited and the Word is not. The Word, if we would allow it, could do miracles through us, just as the Word wrought miracles through the apostles in the early church, but we cannot manipulate the Word or subject it to our will and so do miracles!

The apostles were not high minded, but subject to the Word, believed the Word, in fear, prayer, and humility. They did not attempt to analyze the Word nor did they dilute it with philosophies and worldly knowledge, but received the Word and out of their bellies flowed rivers of living water! The unlimited power flowing through them brought life to dead situations, light to dark places, deliverance to those who were in bondage!

There is no limit to what the Word of God can do through us!

*Now unto him that is able to do exceeding abundantly
above all that we ask or think, according to the power
that worketh in us...*

—Eph. 3:20

SUMMARY

Lord, Plant My Feet On Higher Ground!

THIS *(True Knowledge)* is revelation, i.e., reception of knowledge by the communication (Word) of God, God as the sender and receiver. For He must treat the being with Himself in order for the being to be receptor. Perfect communication. There is no room for error.

THAT *(What the world calls knowledge)* is the reception of knowledge of any kind through any other means, such as empiricism, which is discovery through the experience of the senses.

THIS *(True Knowledge)* is unchanging and sure. *This* within its own definition leaves no place for error for it is initiated and completed by God.

THAT *(What the world calls knowledge)* by its very nature is fallible due to its dubious source, and receptor-interpretation which cannot claim certainty nor even believe in such. There is variableness inherent in concepts established in relativity; therefore conflict and impasse are unavoidable and even reasonable.

THAT *(What the world calls knowledge)* attempts to adapt God's communication to the parameters of the thinking mind. And since God makes it clear in Isaiah chapter 55 that His thoughts are unlike our thoughts, we know that the submission of the Word to human parameters is surely a corruption of that same Word.

THAT *(What the world calls knowledge)* is talking of some person, place or thing "over there."

The mind has parameters (boundaries) that are limits to the infinite Word and when the Word is placed within our understanding it is affected by the shape of the boundaries and therefore corrupted.

THIS *(True Knowledge)* is talking of those things visible and invisible that are here, up close.

Christ the solid rock equals THIS. All other ground equals THAT.
Give us space just to say Hallelujah, Hallelujah, Hallelujah!
Thank you!
On Christ the Solid Rock I Stand!

CHAPTER 3

"On Christ the solid rock I stand. All other ground is sinking sand."

Men Are Willingly Ignorant

Even after being exposed to true knowledge, the Bible speaks of those who are willingly ignorant, scoffing at the Word, walking after their own lusts. These are the people who are not willing to submit, not desiring to receive or acknowledge truth.

> *This second epistle, beloved, I now write unto you; in both which I stir up your pure minds by way of remembrance: That ye may be mindful of the words which were spoken before by the holy prophets, and of the commandment of us the apostles of the Lord and Saviour: Knowing this first, that there shall come in the last days scoffers, walking after their own lusts, And saying, Where is the promise of his coming? for since the fathers fell asleep, all things continue as they were from*

the beginning of the creation. For this they willingly are
ignorant of, that by the word of God the heavens were
of old, and the earth standing out of the water and in
the water: Whereby the world that then was, being
overflowed with water, perished: But the heavens and
the earth, which are now, by the same word are kept
in store, reserved unto fire against the day of judgment
and perdition of ungodly men.

—2 Pet. 3:1-7

There are those who scoff at the idea of God creating the universe and are willfully ignorant, dating the world according to their own timetable, saying, "Where is the promise of his coming?" They do not acknowledge that the Word of God is the authority.

The world is not as it was and they cannot date things their way. The water canopy is not there. The antediluvian world (before the flood) is very much unlike this world therefore the dating beyond that period is not accurate. All the dating we try to do is totally out of line because things do not continue as they were. All we know is a different reality and knowledge than they had. But the scoffers are willingly ignorant of that knowledge, and do not want to acknowledge that the world is totally different now not having a water canopy over it. Based on the water canopy, one day with the lord is as a thousand years....

It has been said that it took 6,000 years to make heaven and earth. But what it really lets us know is that the six days that God had in regulating and setting up the world, he has given man six days to regulate and

"On Christ the solid rock I stand.
All other ground is sinking sand."

rule himself. When man has concluded in destruction in all that is good and right and healthy for him, then we will begin the Sabbath. Six days, six thousand years. He's giving us 6,000 years for six days. And the day of the Lord, the last 1,000 of the 7,000 years shall come as a thief in the night; it will be inaugurated and come to pass suddenly.

Either We Will Believe God, or We Will Have Nothing Worth Believing

John refers to the world's prophets and the world's followers. These are those with humanistic mindsets and humanistic understanding.

They are of the world: therefore speak they of the world, and the world heareth them. We are of God: he that knoweth God heareth us; he that is not of God heareth not us. Hereby know we the Spirit of truth, and the spirit of error.

—1 John 4:5-6

Paul lets us know that God's wisdom confounds the world's prophets and their wisdom.

For the preaching of the cross is to them that perish foolishness; but unto us which are saved it is the power of God. For it is written, I will destroy the wisdom of the wise, and will bring to nothing the understanding of the prudent. Where is the wise? where is the scribe? where is the disputer of this world? hath not God made foolish the wisdom of this world? For after that in the wisdom of God the world by wisdom knew not God, it pleased God by the foolishness of preaching to save them that believe. For the Jews require a sign, and the Greeks seek after wisdom: But we preach Christ crucified, unto the Jews a stumblingblock, and unto the Greeks foolishness; But unto them which are called, both Jews and Greeks, Christ the power of God, and the wisdom of God. Because the foolishness of God is wiser than men; and the weakness of God is stronger than men. For ye see your calling, brethren, how that not many wise men after the flesh, not many mighty, not many noble, are called: But God hath chosen the foolish things of the world to confound the wise; and God hath chosen the weak things of the world to confound the things which are mighty; And base things of the world, and things which are despised, hath God chosen, yea, and things which are not, to bring to nought things that are: That no flesh should glory in his presence. But of him are ye in Christ Jesus, who of God is made unto us wisdom, and righteousness, and sanctification, and redemption: That, according as it is written, He that glorieth, let him glory in the Lord.

—1 Cor. 1:18-31

Howbeit we speak wisdom among them that are perfect: yet not the wisdom of this world, nor of the princes of this world, that come to nought: But we speak the wisdom of God in a mystery, even the hidden wisdom, which God ordained before the world unto our glory: Which none

"On Christ the solid rock I stand.
All other ground is sinking sand."

*of the princes of this world knew: for had they known
it, they would not have crucified the Lord of glory.*
—1 Cor. 2:6-8

Peter also reminds us that we must not be led away by worldly wisdom, but be steadfast, growing in grace and in the knowledge of Jesus Christ.

This second epistle, beloved, I now write unto you; in both which I stir up your pure minds by way of remembrance: That ye may be mindful of the words which were spoken before by the holy prophets, and of the commandment of us the apostles of the Lord and Saviour:
—2 Peter 3:1-2

Nevertheless we, according to his promise, look for new heavens and a new earth, wherein dwelleth righteousness. Wherefore, beloved, seeing that ye look for such things, be diligent that ye may be found of him in peace, without spot, and blameless. And account that the longsuffering of our Lord is salvation; even as our beloved brother Paul also according to the wisdom given unto him hath written unto you; As also in all his epistles, speaking in them of these things; in which are some things hard to be understood, which they that are unlearned and unstable wrest, as they do also the other scriptures, unto their own destruction. Ye therefore, beloved, seeing ye know these things before, beware lest ye also, being led away with the error of the wicked, fall from your own stedfastness. But grow in grace, and in the knowledge of our Lord and Saviour Jesus Christ. To him be glory both now and for ever. Amen.

—2 Peter 3:13-18

The Word of God as Definer, the Final Authority

We know that the Word is alive and powerful but *you must make yourself available* to the Word. We cannot say this enough.

It's not about how hard you concentrate your mental faculties to break it down, but it's about how available you make yourself to it. For one to make oneself available to the Word, as opposed to wrestling the Word down, seeking to *obtain* its treasures, is a matter of spiritual attitude. If your attitude is that the Word is merely information, then that is offensive to Him.

Do you not know that God's Word is able to tell you things, show you things? Have you ever looked at something and then allowed the Word to define it for you from the inside of you? Have you asked the Word, "What is that or why is that?" and you look at it through the Word and you understand it differently? That is revelation!

If you will have the Word as guide and interpreter of this world you shall never stumble nor trip. Jesus is the Word. Jesus is the Light. If He abides in us He said we would not stumble. In order for the Word to be powerful in us we must recognize it as the prime and final authority for interpreting reality in our lives that we might walk according to truth.

"On Christ the solid rock I stand.
All other ground is sinking sand."

This is not an astounding new truth. Christians have known this and have been blessed by this since our first knowledge in the Lord. But what I am proposing is that we are stunted in our growth because we only receive that which our brain can reach. It is therefore true without a doubt *that the foolishness of God is wiser than men; and the weakness of God is stronger than men (1 Corinthians 1:25).*

The Word speaks of itself as alive and powerful, which means we must cease from scrutinizing and analyzing the Word with an intent to retrieve its content by force of intellect. We analyze the Word and dissect it as opposed to covering ourselves with the Word and allowing it access to process our perception.

We must allow the Word to enter in and process us. We must allow revelation to come from the Word and subject ourselves to the Word. The Word is the greater. We will not process it but it will process us. The problem is that we attempt to do just the opposite and this is why we don't receive from the Word. This is why we're limited in our knowledge of the Word.

If you abide in me and my words abide in you, you shall ask what you will and it shall be given unto you.
—John 15:7

One who abides in the Word has a promise that God will give unto him according to his request. If they take the Word in and dissect it and don't understand it with their human mindset, I believe that there are some vestiges they will receive with the Word.

I believe that even if we take the Word by force we still receive something, but it can be distorted by the motivations of our forcing. It is the will of the Word that we should know it, but when we exert our own mental pressure we pollute the Word by what we bring to it. And many times we come to the Word with preconceived notions and pre-scripted expectations and we get what we expect instead of what is there. The result is corrupted outcome, which for all intents and purposes is a lie.

Knowledge is the content of truth. If it is not true knowledge then it is not knowledge at all. It is for this cause that the Holy Spirit in the Word is hampered and humans come away from the Word with humanistic corruptions and say that the Word is self-conflicting or that it is fallible. A man without truth thinks that he has knowledge.

The Word is not fallible but the human mind that believes that it can extract true content by its own will focused upon the Word is fallible. The human mind having believed that it has beheld fallibility in the Word then says that there are many ways of understanding the Word. This is a common humanistic failure blamed on the Word.

CHAPTER 4

The Hindered Flow

What is Blocking the Flow?

I f we truly have a desire to receive from the Word with an honest heart, we will receive from Him. Any interaction with the Word of God from an honest heart is bound to bring forth to some extent. For one may be incorrect without being wrong. We believe that many are simply ignorant without intending to be disobedient. Hearing the Word of God will deliver one from accidental ignorance. Hopefully, it will bring many to repentance who have heard the Word and failed to be still and submitted, that they might have revelation.

The Word cannot flow because it is strangulated, constricting the flow. The Word is being choked, or suppressed.

When we bring our knowledge we restrict the flow and we only receive trickles of revelational knowledge. We must come empty. The flow is restricted when we are not empty, attempting to make Him available to us instead of humbly bowing to receive the engrafted Word. The Word cannot flow into an already full vessel!

We are not seeking to put the Word of God into a mold, but allowing the Word to mold us. We're not attempting to master the Word of God, but our desire is that it should master us.

When I come and submit myself to the Word then I am making myself available to Him. Once I recognize that it is a fearful, living being, then the flow of the Holy Spirit is enabled by my faith and by my right attitude to bring forth powerfully in me, by me, through me.

Pride is a primary hindrance. Pride is the grace impediment. As we have indicated before, pride enfeebles the church. It besets the saints. When we are prideful, the Word is hindered from enduing us to our maximum capacity. God resists the proud and gives more grace to the humble.

What is pride? Loving ourselves more than God is the base of pride, and causes us to impede the Holy Spirit and bring destruction on ourselves.

Pride shows itself in our leaning to our own understanding and by our giving primacy to our intelligence and emotional comprehension as opposed to acknowledging the Word of God that was given by the Holy Ghost. In other words, when we think we know and don't seek the Word of God, we hinder the Holy Spirit. In effect this is a form of blasphemy when we lift anything in our imagination above the knowledge of God.

Pride has many offsprings. Anger comes by pride. Anger absorbs our total focus, causing us not to be subject to the Holy Spirit; therefore we are brought to the point that we impede the work of the Holy Spirit in us.

Self-seeking, seeking promotion, and ambitiously seeking approval of the world compromises our self-examining and honesty, which causes us by pride to impede the Holy Spirit.

Hatred, jealousy and fear, stem from pride, and through these a person comes to bitterness, and bitterness impedes the Holy Spirit. Hebrews 12:15 says, *"Looking diligently lest any man fail of the grace of God; lest any root of bitterness springing up trouble you, and thereby many be defiled;"*

Unto the pure all things are pure: but unto them that are defiled and unbelieving is nothing pure; but even their mind and conscience is defiled. They profess that they know God; but in works they deny him, being abominable, and disobedient, and unto every good work reprobate.

—Titus 1:15-16

Then Jesus said unto his disciples, If any man will come after me, let him deny himself, and take up his cross, and follow me. For whosoever will save his life shall lose it: and whosoever will lose his life for my sake shall find it. For what is a man profited, if he shall gain the whole world, and lose his own soul? or what shall a man give in exchange for his soul?

—Matt. 16:24-26

Blasphemy of the Holy Ghost consists of such things as ignoring His divinity and right to instruct us and to ignore the wisdom and help of His teaching.

And whosoever shall speak a Word against the Son of man, it shall be forgiven him: but unto him that blasphemeth against the Holy Ghost it shall not be forgiven.

—Luke 12:10

But the Comforter, which is the Holy Ghost, whom the Father will send in my name, he shall teach you all things, and bring all things to your remembrance, whatsoever I have said unto you.

—John 14:26

Seeing that it is the job of the Holy Spirit to teach us the Word of Christ and to teach us all things, if we should blaspheme (as defined above) Him then how shall we know the way of salvation or how else shall we receive revelation? The impediment to revelation is to hinder the work of the Holy Spirit.

Unbelief is that quality that brings retardation to the new creature in Christ.

He (the Word) did not many mighty works there because of their unbelief.

—Matt. 13:58

God has limited himself to respond to faith. Faith in its purest and simplest terms is to believe God's Word.

So the failure to believe God resulted in God pulling back from the works that had been seen in many other areas of Palestine. The Galilean area was Jesus' home place. The people of Galilee believed that they were on familiar terms with the miracle working Word of God, whom they saw as Jesus, the son of the carpenter from their own neighborhood. By their knowledge they were puffed up and failed to receive a revelation of His wonder working power.

In the same way, those who believe that they can by discovery become familiar with the Word of God, stem the flow of His revelation by their unbelief for He has made it known that His Word lives, imparts life and is powerful and is a discerner of our physical and spiritual depths.

We don't need to try to discover what God is so willing to reveal, but we must be mindful not to be abusive to this being called the Word of God. We must be respectful and know that He is the Son of God.

Our problem is that we seek by forceful interrogation to cause the Word to submit to our minds, rather than to submit and plead to Him. By reading and hearing in meekness and humility, we make ourselves available by faith to receive revelation. Again, God resists the proud and gives grace to the lowly

Attempting to wrangle the Word out

And Jacob was left alone; and there wrestled a man with him until the breaking of the day. And when he saw that he prevailed not against him, he touched the

hollow of his thigh; and the hollow of Jacob's thigh was
out of joint, as he wrestled with him. And he said, Let
me go, for the day breaketh. And he said, I will not let
thee go, except thou bless me.

—Gen. 32:24

Why is it that this man (the presence of God) was unable to overcome Jacob, but yet had the capacity or the power to merely touch him and cripple him for the rest of his life? What if he had touched him in his head or in his chest? I believe that he would have doubtlessly killed him. The reason that he wrestled is because he refused to render Jacob unable to fulfill God's future will. Jacob refused to let go. So that it was mercy that sustained Jacob and it was Jacob's crude man-like behavior that caused the presence of God to have mercy upon Jacob's insistence, and He wanted to depart from Jacob before Jacob could see His face in the light of day, for no man can see the face of God and live. Exodus 33:20 reads, "*And he said, Thou canst not see my face: for there shall no man see me, and live.*"

It was grace that allowed Jacob to wrestle and to beg a blessing. It was goodness and love on the part of God that allowed Jacob his blessing. Jacob was still not right in his heart, which is why his encounter with God was one of contention.

Samuel, on the other hand, was called and answered saying, "Here am I, speak, for thy servant heareth" (1 Samuel 3:10). Samuel was enabled to receive greater blessing and revelation than his forerunner and father,

Jacob. Samuel humbly received guidance from his teacher, Eli, and was therefore prepared to approach the Lord in humility. A prepared heart and mind will approach God not with intent to wring truth from Him, but to present himself/herself before God and be humble and receptive and so receive God's revelation.

Also, remember Isaiah who made himself available and was thus commissioned by revelation of God.

> *Also I heard the voice of the Lord, saying, Whom shall I send, and who will go for us? Then said I, Here am I; send me.*
>
> —Isa. 6:8

Operating out of our own understanding

> *Trust in the LORD with all thine heart; and lean not unto thine own understanding.*
>
> —Prov. 3:5

Emotion is our motive for moving or doing. I cannot move out of my own understanding. Emotions are the primary motivators of humanity. Feelings are the key to our motivations. Whatever affects your emotions becomes your master. Satan affects the emotions. In all our ways we should acknowledge God and obey Him and not our own feelings or understanding.

We are beings made to be enslaved. We were created and made to be servants to work for God. Being a slave is not a bad thing. A slave is someone who works for someone else. We were created to be obedient.

We must obey God and not walk after our own feelings. We are to walk by faith and not by sight.

Approaching God with wrong mindset

When you approach God and approach the Word what do you think you're doing? Do you want God to stimulate your mental apparatus by the Word? And what difference would that make?

When we approach God with all the issues of evolution and psychology for learning, we approach God with a high-mindedness approach that God resists. That's why we come away from the Word unmoved and without power. Because we sought to approach it in our high-mindedness and God resists us.

We cannot come to understand that spirituality and intelligence often are vying with each other. We know that Lucifer was the cherub who was very intelligent and high-minded, desiring those things that belonged only to God. When people get intelligent they are hard, they are cold and distant, and are not nigh unto God. God is not near because God is nigh unto them with a broken heart and a contrite Spirit. Jesus told the father in a prayer in Matthew 11:25, *"I thank thee, O Father, Lord of heaven and earth, because thou hast hid these things from the wise and prudent, and hast revealed them unto babes."*

If you know a lot, especially if your knowing is not by revelation, if your knowing is because you're smart, let he who thinks he knows become as a fool. Throw that down so that you can get to know God.

Some people think they're more street smart, more intelligent, have higher IQ's. Spiritual wisdom has nothing to do with any of that, in fact that gets in the way. When God reveals, that's when we know. God's revelation is true knowledge!

Whatever you think you have that makes you brighter than the rest, such as a high IQ, education, street smarts, come down, come down! You pollute the Word. If you're bright and smart you will always be about analyzing the Word and never getting it. Don't behave with God like that. Don't approach Him like that!

Man informs man that he is high, that he has reached the height of his endeavor, but he is really one who is starving for God. One who approaches with humility, begging the Word for revelation, making himself subject, waiting, trusting, down low before the Word of God, it is he into whom God pours his own wisdom by revelation.

I don't believe that there is any school that is able to do that unless the instructor explains to the student that they have to wait on God to get this, because that student is not going to get it due to academic prowess; he can't discover or unlock God's Word, he's not going to do that if he approaches it academically. If we want to be powerful, then we must approach the Word in terms of availability. That's why there is a need for institutes of availability established in the churches everywhere with a humbleness toward the Word of God. Revelational knowledge. Not academic knowledge, but revelational knowledge.

We are supposed to get humble under the Word. That's why those who understand this are not impressed by academics and the world.

It's a matter of attitude. God resists anyone who approaches Him with a know-it-all and high-minded attitude. *You're not going to unlock anything.*

CHAPTER 5

There's Water in the Rock!

The Treasures of the Word: More Precious Than Silver, Gold, and Jewels

> *My son, if thou wilt receive my words, and hide my commandments with thee;*
>
> —Prov. 2:1

> *So that thou incline thine ear unto wisdom, and apply thine heart to understanding;*
>
> —Prov. 2:2

> *Happy is the man that findeth wisdom, and the man that getteth understanding. For the merchandise of it is better than the merchandise of silver, and the gain thereof than fine gold. She is more precious than rubies: and all the things thou canst desire are not to be compared unto her.*
>
> —Prov. 3:13

There is gold, and a multitude of rubies: but the lips of knowledge are a precious jewel.

—Prov. 20:15

Yea, if thou criest after knowledge, and liftest up thy voice for understanding; If thou seekest her as silver, and searchest for her as for hid treasures; Then shalt thou understand the fear of the LORD, and find the knowledge of God, For the LORD giveth wisdom: out of his mouth cometh knowledge and understanding.

—Prov. 2:3

I f thou seekest her and searcheth for her—this is prayer! The Bible talks about asking and seeking, and in so doing it is describing an active prayer life. Here we talk about seeking and searching and again we are talking about seeking unto God, searching the boundaries of His favor to have our needs met. The gold and the silver is merely speaking of those things which are precious and if we recognize how precious the desired treasure is we will surely seek from our heavenly Father that He will be gracious and give to us that which He has shown us is precious.

We don't obtain wisdom, but God giveth wisdom. The Lord giveth, that's how we come to wisdom and understanding. We have no reason to brag.

That no flesh should glory in his presence.

—1 Cor. 1:29

For who maketh thee to differ from another? and what hast thou that thou didst not receive? now if thou didst receive it, why dost thou glory, as if thou hadst not received it?

—1 Cor 4:7

In other words it is not *obtained,* which speaks of our capacities and faculties and efforts that result in achievement, but it is of a kind and merciful Father who by His Word *giveth* every good and perfect gift.

Every good gift and every perfect gift is from above, and cometh down from the Father of lights, with whom is no variableness, neither shadow of turning.

—James 1: 17

He that spared not his own Son, but delivered him up for us all, how shall he not with him also freely give us all things?

—Rom. 8:32 32

Now we have received, not the spirit of the world, but the Spirit which is of God; that we might know the things that are freely given to us of God.

—1 Cor. 2:12

So then faith cometh by hearing, and hearing by the word of God.

—Rom. 10:17

The wisdom that God gives us is faith. And faith comes by the Word of God.

For unto us was the gospel preached, as well as unto them: but the word preached did not profit them, not being mixed with faith in them that heard it.
—Heb. 4:2

The Word itself is unlocked by the wisdom that God gives and the wisdom itself is faith, not works, so that no one can boast.

But God hath chosen the foolish things of the world to confound the wise; and God hath chosen the weak things of the world to confound the things which are mighty; And base things of the world, and things which are despised, hath God chosen, yea, and things which are not, to bring to nought things that are: That no flesh should glory in his presence.
—1 Cor. 1:27

For I know that in me (that is, in my flesh,) dwelleth no good thing: for to will is present with me; but how to perform that which is good I find not.
—Rom. 7:18

But without faith it is impossible to please him: for he that cometh to God must believe that he is, and that he is a rewarder of them that diligently seek him.
—Heb. 11:6

By the Word He instills faith and by faith we seek Him, but He is the rewarder of our faith. So even faith is not the final rewarder but faith in God gives Him pleasure and He responds to us with knowledge and wisdom. Diligently seeking Him is the same as making ourselves available to the Word by hearing, believing, by reading and meditating. And the Word reveals....

His Word is Spirit. His Spirit is truth.

The precious treasures are flowing down from the mouth of God, is there anyone prepared to receive?

> *And the LORD came, and stood, and called as at other times, Samuel, Samuel. Then Samuel answered, Speak; for thy servant heareth.*
>
> —1 Sam. 3:10

Receiving the Full Flow!

God's desire is that we know Him—not merely become acquainted with Him, but to know Him. The only way that we are able to know Him is through the living Word of God. *There is no other way!* As much as we are available, He extends Himself to us. As much as we seek Him to hear and receive His Word, He reveals Himself to us. His Word is His expression. God desires to fill us with His Word. He wants to pour into us. God's desire is that His Word dwell in us richly. It is important that we do not hinder the flow of His disclosure by our own content. We must set aside anything that exalts itself against the knowledge of Him.

There is a difference between knowing of someone and actually knowing that person. The difference is that to know of someone, you may have heard of someone else's experience with that person, or read about that person. However, to know someone is to have personal knowledge from the person, which involves spending time with, communicating with, and learning about that person. This can only be done if the person who would learn can silence his own internal verbiage and be totally receptive to the one who is revealing himself.

When we are subject to Him and have a relationship with Him, He communicates with us. Jesus says in John 15:14:15 *"Henceforth I call you not servants; for the servant knoweth not what his lord doeth: but I have called you friends; for all things that I have heard of my Father I have made known unto you."*

Job was God's servant. In God's discourse with Job, his response to God as recorded in Job 42:5 was, *"I have heard of thee by the hearing of the ear: but now mine eye seeth thee."* Job was saying, Now my spiritual eyes are open and I can see you. I not only see what you're doing, but now I know your ways, you have revealed yourself to me and I have received! The Lord works in mysterious ways, His wonders to perform!

Remember the passages in Luke 24:13-35, when the two who went to Emmaus were discussing the crucifixion and the empty tomb? They were saddened and had no understanding of what had taken place. Jesus drew nigh to them and expounded, that is, He gave them understanding in all the Scriptures of the things concerning himself. They asked Him to abide with them and He tarried with them. They supped with Jesus. Their eyes were opened, and they knew Him; and He vanished out of their sight. And they said one to another; *"Did not our heart burn within us, while he talked with us by the way, and while he opened to us the scriptures? "*

> *Behold, I stand at the door, and knock: if any man hear my voice, and open the door, I will come in to him, and will sup with him, and he with me.*
>
> —Rev. 3:20

We can't even begin to fathom the knowledge that God has stored up for those who love him. The treasures of the Word that we receive in our Spirit, when He communicates His Word to us, causes us to understand, opens up the Word in to our Spirit!

> *But as it is written, Eye hath not seen, nor ear heard, neither have entered into the heart of man, the things which God hath prepared for them that love him. But God hath revealed them unto us by his Spirit: for the Spirit searcheth all things, yea, the deep things of God*
>
> —1 Cor. 2:9

We have grown accustomed to receiving trickles or drops of revelation from God, here and there, but God's desire is that His Word, by revelation, flow to us and through us.

We receive the full flow when we bow down and pray, "Teach me Lord!"

We, ourselves, hinder the life-giving flow of His Word because of what we bring to the reception. We come with content when we should come as an empty pitcher before a full fountain. When we attempt by what we know and by content of our mental capability to know spiritual things, we err and color the truth. Our understanding clouds the way. We project our own understanding and thought upon the Word, and then receive that same projection unto ourselves, believing that we have received the unadulterated Word of God. We don't realize that we are seeking ourselves and calling it God. It were better that we would say, "I don't understand, Lord, help me," than to define God's Word in terms of ourselves. Colored truth is no truth at all.

Revelational knowledge must be used. Allow the Word to work on you. Hear God's Word; listen to Him. Become doers of that knowledge. Humbly make yourself available to the Word, and then through faith appropriate those things.

The process of sanctification is submitting under the Word of God. The Word will yield knowledge; we don't press for knowledge or attain to knowledge by our own will but it is a gift.

We have to be somewhere where God can make deposits into us. We must intentionally come before the Word, come into His presence. Instead of attempting to bring the Word into our presence, we must come before His presence, submitting to the Word instead of attempting to have the Word submit to us. He is the King of Glory!

Now be ye not stiffnecked, as your fathers were, but yield yourselves unto the LORD, and enter into his sanctuary, which he hath sanctified for ever: and serve

the LORD your God, that the fierceness of his wrath
may turn away from you.
—2 Chron. 30:8 (KJV)

We receive the unhindered flow of knowledge for our Spiritual life by intentionally making ourselves available for reception, sitting under the Word, seeking the Word, and hearkening to the Word.

And, behold, I send the promise of my Father upon you:
but tarry ye in the city of Jerusalem, until ye be endued
with power from on high.
—Luke 24:49

The disciples intentionally made themselves available and the Word came and spoke with them and endued them with power and knowledge.

Come before the Lord in fear and humility. In order to receive the treasures of the Word, the full, unhindered flow of revelational knowledge, God's reproving insists that we must change our attitudes in approaching His Word. We have stated that often we approach His Word as if by the power of our minds we can manipulate it and take from His Word its hidden treasure. The error is shown in that we fail to receive the Word's treasure. We must be fearful enough to change and submit, and be in place to humbly receive God's blessings.

We must have a fearfulness for the Word of God, and an attitude of reverence, not seeking to manipulate the Word but waiting in faith for the Word to speak to us.

The fear of the Lord is the beginning of wisdom and knowledge. Why would we think that we could approach the living Word of God without fear? The Word that we give to all is: Fear God in every revealed manifestation. Academia does not approach the Word with an attitude of fear but with an attitude of superiority of mind in which it seeks to submit the Word to its analytical capabilities. This is an insult to almighty God who has already informed us that we will not know Him by discovery but by His own revelation to us.

> *For who maketh thee to differ from another? and what hast thou that thou didst not receive? now if thou didst receive it, why dost thou glory, as if thou hadst not received it?*
>
> —1 Cor. 4:7 (KJV)

> *Who is this that cometh from Edom, with dyed garments from Bozrah? this that is glorious in his apparel, travelling in the greatness of his strength? I that speak in righteousness, mighty to save. Wherefore art thou red in thine apparel, and thy garments like him that treadeth in the winefat? I have trodden the winepress alone; and of the people there was none with me: for I will tread them in mine anger, and trample them in my fury; and their blood shall be sprinkled upon my garments, and I will stain all my raiment. For the day of vengeance is in mine heart, and the year of my redeemed is come. And I looked, and there was none to help; and I wondered that there was none to uphold: therefore mine own arm brought salvation unto me; and my fury, it upheld me.*

And I will tread down the people in mine anger, and make them drunk in my fury, and I will bring down their strength to the earth.

—Isa. 63:1-6 (KJV)

He that rejecteth me, and receiveth not my words, hath one that judgeth him: the word that I have spoken, the same shall judge him in the last day.

—John 12:48

And he was clothed with a vesture dipped in blood: and his name is called The Word of God. And the armies which were in heaven followed him upon white horses, clothed in fine linen, white and clean. And out of his mouth goeth a sharp sword, that with it he should smite the nations: and he shall rule them with a rod of iron: and he treadeth the winepress of the fierceness and wrath of Almighty God.

—Rev. 19:13-15

This is the Word of God. Don't approach Him as if you can find Him out. The Bible tells us that you can't find God out. Approach in humility!

Touching the Almighty, we cannot find him out: he is excellent in power, and in judgment, and in plenty of justice: he will not afflict. Men do therefore fear him: he respecteth not any that are wise of heart.

—Job 37:23-24

He hath made every thing beautiful in his time: also he hath set the world in their heart, so that no man can find out the work that God maketh from the beginning to the end.

—Eccles. 3:11

For after that in the wisdom of God the world by wisdom knew not God, it pleased God by the foolishness of preaching to save them that believe.

—1 Cor. 1:21

He that rejecteth me, and receiveth not my words, hath one that judgeth him: the Word that I have spoken, the same shall judge him in the last day.

—John 12:48

We must recognize the Word as Himself, God. By approaching the Word as those who are subject to it and known by it we will not be haughty or high-minded but meek, humble and highly blessed in our own experience. So is fulfilled the Word which says that He gives grace to the humble.

Seek to receive what the Word has to impart to you. Do not attempt to dissect or break the Word down, it is impossible to do so. The Word is bigger than we are.

Somehow the church has over the years had the misconception that by our effort and by our IQ we could wring from God the sweet treasures of wisdom. For we have not recognized that God's Word is that which God has sent to accomplish *(Isaiah 55)* nor have we understood that His Word is alive and powerful, a discerner of the very depths of our physical, spiritual being. We have set out in the *greatness* of our perceived mentality *(Prov 3:7:1 "Be not wise in thine own eyes: fear the LORD, and depart from evil")* to dissect and analyze the Word of almighty God, which Word is God.

When we approach the Word in total surrender, He can do His work in us, molding and rearranging our thoughts, attitudes and deeds. We must submit to the Word of God and be broken.

When we do approach in fear and humility as prescribed by the Word of God, the initiation into this process becomes, by divine plan and implementation, *faithful hearing,* the result of which is reception of knowledge in the Spirit-man.

> *He that hath an ear, let him hear what the Spirit saith unto the churches.*
> —Rev. 3: 22

Listen, hearken to the Word. Listen to the voice of God when He enters in.

May the Lord have mercy on our souls for our fearlessness and our haughtiness of mind.

Confess our sins and be cleansed by His blood. When we come before the Lord, we are unable to enter into the inner court until we have confessed our sins to Him who is able to cleanse us from all unrighteousness, the Word of God. The Word washes us and is able to present us faultless. Honestly confess; the Word is a discerner of the thoughts and intents of the heart.

If we confess our sins, he is faithful and just to forgive us our sins, and to cleanse us from all unrighteousness.

—1 John 1:10

If we say that we have not sinned, we make him a liar, and his word is not in us.

—1 John 1:9

Thus saith the Lord GOD; No stranger, uncircumcised in heart, nor uncircumcised in flesh, shall enter into my sanctuary, of any stranger that is among the children of Israel.

—Ezek. 44:9 (KJV)

And it shall come to pass, that when they enter in at the gates of the inner court, they shall be clothed with linen garments; and no wool shall come upon them, whiles they minister in the gates of the inner court, and within.

—Ezek. 44:17 (KJV)

Neither shall any priest drink wine, when they enter into the inner court.

—Ezek. 44:21 (KJV)

And in the day that he goeth into the sanctuary, unto the inner court, to minister in the sanctuary, he shall offer his sin offering, saith the Lord GOD.

—Ezek. 44:27 (KJV)

We must sing His praises and be glad in our hearts that we are enabled to come into His presence by the blood and love of His own Son. We know that He is not in any wise reluctant for He has done all, that we might have access unto Himself.

> *Enter into his gates with thanksgiving, and into his courts with praise: be thankful unto him, and bless his name.*
>
> —Ps. 100:4 (KJV)

> *So the Spirit took me up, and brought me into the inner court; and, behold, the glory of the LORD filled the house.*
>
> —Ezek. 43:5

Remembering that God resists the proud, let us humble ourselves in our own sight and magnify Him in our focused attention to appreciate, to thank, and to love Him, esteeming Him above all, adoring Him in gladness and joy. We will see His glory, His splendor, His Honor.

We Must Expect To Receive From God by Faith.

Jesus asked the two blind men who cried out for Him to have mercy on them (Matthew 9:27-29) "Believe ye that I am able to do this? They answered, Yes Lord! Jesus touched their eyes and said according to your faith be it unto you and their eyes were opened!"

Hear Him, Be Open to Him and Receive into our Hearts, the Mighty Word of God, *Christ the King, Himself!* Rev 3:20 reads, *"Behold, I stand at the door, and knock: if any man hear my voice, and open the door, I will come in to him, and will sup with him, and he with me."*

Jeremiah said, The word of the Lord came unto me saying....

When we open our hearts to the Word in faith, reception takes place. Reception is that which is received, in this case spiritual revelation. When we receive the Word it produces a living thing within us. That living thing is planted and grows in us. The problem is not the lack of the gift of knowledge, but a lack of the reception of knowledge. God freely gives knowledge. Whether we will meekly be in reception directly affects the quality and fullness of the flow of spiritual knowledge into our Spirit-man. But we have understood the need of fear. God has plainly told us but we have been disobedient and had rather walk in the light of our pride and human mentality.

> *For the word of God is quick, and powerful, and sharper than any twoedged sword, piercing even to the dividing asunder of soul and Spirit, and of the joints and marrow, and is a discerner of the thoughts and intents of the heart. Neither is there any creature that is not manifest in his sight: but all things are naked and opened unto the eyes of him with whom we have to do.*
>
> —Heb. 4:12-13

There can be no superior attitude when a subject has an audience with the King.

When we are open to the Word and allow Him entrance, we humbly submit to Him, as a host who has the privilege of receiving the King of Glory into his own home. We bow our hearts down in humble homage to the great King and in reverence receive from Him. When He visits us, we sup with Him and He with us. He imparts the treasures. He quenches our thirst, the water flows freely, there is an abundance of the bread of life. We will dine together with Him. This is the everlasting covenant.

We must not let any high thing, thought, or imagination that lifts itself against the knowledge of God, bar His entry. Whatever blocks the flow must be cast down. He is the almighty Word of God, full of light and truth. He will manifest, show forth, reveal Himself in us and to us. Hearken to what the Word of God reveals.

How do we submit, how do we humble ourselves, how can we be meek? In our spirit, we must be still and attentive. In our spirit, in our mind, in our heart, we must be still and know. And we will know by his revelation if we be still.

The Word of God is alive and gives life!

When does the Word of God become alive? The Word of God becomes alive to us when He enters into our heart, when He is received in, when we are born again. This is what makes us different from bibliolotry (the worship of the Bible). We do not worship the Bible. We know that the Bible is a book. The Word is alive when we receive the Word into our hearts.

The Word enters in and when we receive Him in faith, He changes us.

Engrafting is when a foreign branch is placed into the root and stock of another plant, into a cut made in the plant, and is able to grow there even though it was not a part of that original plant.

In Romans 11, Paul talks about how we were grafted in. This means when the split was made scion is placed into that split and is able to grow even though it is not germane to the stock that it was put into. We were grafted into the Jewish blessings that God promised to Abraham and his children, and we became members of the commonwealth of Israel, the children of Abraham, who is our father in the faith.

Now we're talking about the Word that is foreign because it is spiritual and we are flesh. The Word is engrafted and we are born spirit in the engraft and are the children of God because of that which was grafted in. There is another thing that we have to remember about graft, that it has kinship with *graph*. *Graph* means to scratch, etch, by use of a stylus, which means that by the scratching and the stylus writing took place and hence the word *graph*. In that sense it has to do with writing something within us as God said that He would write His Word upon the table stones of our hearts. So this word *engraft* is for us rich with meaning.

The engrafted Word, the Word written within us and foreign to us is, by the divine operation of God, implanted into an inferior host. But it becomes greater than its host in that Spirit is superior to the flesh. This is how a new creature is born from above.

Wherefore lay apart all filthiness and superfluity of naughtiness, and receive with meekness the engrafted Word, which is able to save your souls.

—James 1:21

We receive with meekness the engrafted Word, understanding that we are carnal and we are humbly blessed by the incoming Word, which is eternal and spiritual. Knowing that the inferior should be grateful to be included by miracle into things that are spiritual, we realize what a loving God He is to allow us to receive of Him!

What is it that makes that place for the Word to be engrafted in? What makes that split in us for the Word to be grafted? We can only say that it is hearing according to the Word of God.

What makes us able to hear at that point is divine intervention and divine operation—things too wonderful for us. We can only know that our God is an awesome God.

It's the living Word Himself. Nothing happens to the flesh, but the living Word Himself. He is our birth. It is the seed of our new existence, of the new creature, the new child of God; the Word is the seed. The Word is quick, living and powerful and has within itself the means of our birth; sent from God with purpose, it accomplishes what God sent it to perform. So we are born from above by the Word of God. It is past our capacity to find out, to discover, or analyze. It is spiritual, it is infinite, and it is beyond the comprehension of our gray matter. We can only receive of the knowledge by the Spirit and it is ineffable, unspeakable, incapable of being expressed, but by the Spirit to the spirit.

When We Open The Door, The Word of God Shines the Light In Our Hearts

For God, who commanded the light to shine out of darkness, hath shined in our hearts, to give the light of the knowledge of the glory of God in the face of Jesus Christ.

—2 Cor. 4:6

Jesus says, "Behold I stand at the door and knock." Before we receive Him we are dark, hopeless. He is as a stranger, someone whom we have heard of, talked about, spoke of, read about, but He is not our life, He is not our Lord. Behold, I stand at the door and knock. We are in need of Him, yet He knocks at our heart. Before we come to salvation we will not allow Him to come in. His desire is to come in and fellowship, sup with us. We are dark, thirsty, naked, hungry, and lonely, and yet, He stands outside knocking.

When we open the door of our hearts, the light of the Word exposes and dispels the darkness and overcomes the hopelessness. Life overcomes death. *If we are totally surrendered, the flow is unhindered!*

Neither is there any creature that is not manifest in his sight: but all things are naked and opened unto the eyes of him with whom we have to do.

—Heb. 4:13

Although she may not have realized it, the woman at the well was spiritually thirsty and dry. She stood before the fountain, not acknowledging that she was needy. Her attitude and sins had blinded her and restricted the flow. She knew that the Messiah would come and she even spoke of him, but *she did not know Him.* However, Jesus the Word of God knew who she was and continued to speak to her situation, continued to knock. He was able to shine the light directly into those dark areas, past the facades, behind the mask of the hurt, cutting through her stony heart. He performed surgery right there at the well, removing the blockage. She became an empty pitcher before a full free–flowing fountain. When Jesus, the Word of God, said "I that speak unto thee am He," the woman received the flow of the revelation of who Jesus is, and her life was changed forever.

> *"The entrance of thy words giveth light; it giveth understanding unto the simple."*
> —Ps. 119:130

How do you deal with the light? What do you do with light? What do you attain or strive to get in so far as light is concerned? There is one thing that you can do in regards to the light. One thing is to get in its way and let it shine on you and to take it up that it may shine on all things. But you cannot subject the light to your dark mind and come forth seeing truth. Your mind is empty and bereft of *true* knowledge and darkened by the lie. The only possibility for your mind to be filled with light is that you intentionally make it available to light, refusing to hide in the shadow.

Light is active, powerful, life, an overcomer, and is never overcome by what would appear to be its opposite. But light does not in fact have a true opposite. There is light and there is lack of light and that's all. Lack of light is not an entity. Lack of light is not something that is or can exist. It is simply absence of light. Darkness is not. It is naught. Life, Love, Truth, Spirit, Eternity itself is synonymous with Light. God is light and in Him there is no darkness at all. So of all those things mentioned, only they exist; their opposites do not exist. There is no entity. Darkness cannot come upon light and cause it to flee. But light can shoo away the darkness. Lie cannot come upon truth and expel it. But truth can expel the lie at all points, at all times. There is no opposite in truth. There is no entity that is opposed or can be opposed to these things. If anything would appear to do so, it is an illusion and a lie itself. Satan is a liar and the father of it, therefore he himself is naughty. Proverbs 21:30 says, "There is no wisdom nor understanding nor counsel against the LORD."

Jesus, the light of the world is life; he saves, reveals, teaches, exposes, corrects, guides, delivers, heals, tears down the lies.

This I say therefore, and testify in the Lord, that ye henceforth walk not as other Gentiles walk, in the vanity of their mind, Having the understanding darkened, being alienated from the life of God through the ignorance that is in them, because of the blindness of their heart:

—Ephesians 4:17, 18

CHAPTER 6

We Must Believe the Word!

Faith cometh by hearing and hearing by the Word of God. I can't hear the Word of God except *by* the Word of God, who is alive. So it is that He, the Word of God, somehow must bring me to the Word of God so that I can hear the Word of God, believe the Word of God and be transformed within, born of the Word of God. The Word of God builds faith.

It becomes evident that faith cometh by hearing, and hearing by the Word of God.

> *So then faith cometh by hearing, and hearing by the word of God.*
>
> —Rom. 10:17

> *Through faith we understand that the worlds were framed by the word of God, so that things which are seen were not made of things which do appear.*
>
> —Heb. 11:3

Temporal things are seen by the carnal eye in the carnal mind and spiritual things are seen by Spiritual beings.

> *For unto us was the gospel preached, as well as unto them: but the word preached did not profit them, not being mixed with faith in them that heard it. Faith by the divine operation of God in the Word of God brings forth the child of God, a spiritual creature, and by faith he is nurtured in the Word of God to maturity.*
> —Heb. 4:2

So that even the Word of God *cannot* be discerned by human reasoning, but by the revelation of God through faith. God reveals to us through our faith, and by this we have knowledge.

The mixture of faith upon the Word of God is what profits a person. The Word has to be mixed with faith in order for us to be profited with revelation from God. So that knowledge is the gain wherewith we are profited, and out of that (revelation) comes our total relationship with the Father, for revelation is alive, the Word is alive, and we are spiritually alive by the living communication from our Father. It is the Word that gives me quality of life. All is born out of the admixture of the Word and faith and that not of ourselves, it is a gift of God.

> *God forbid: yea, let God be true, but every man a liar; as it is written, That thou mightest be justified in thy sayings, and mightest overcome when thou art judged.*
> —Rom. 3:4

We Must Believe the Word!

If we believe the Word it will show up in our walk. Our faith shows up when we are not only hearers of the Word, but doers of the Word.

For unto us was the gospel preached, as well as unto them: but the word preached did not profit them, not being mixed with faith in them that heard it.
—Heb. 4:2

And, behold, there cometh one of the rulers of the synagogue, Jairus by name; and when he saw him, he fell at his feet, And besought him greatly, saying, My little daughter lieth at the point of death: I pray thee, come and lay thy hands on her, that she may be healed; and she shall live. And Jesus went with him; and much people followed him, and thronged him.
—Mark 5:22-24

Jairus, one of the rulers of the synagogue, did not approach Jesus with a high-minded attitude, but in humility he fell at His feet. He begged Jesus to come heal his daughter who was at the point of death. As they walked, can you imagine how Jairus must have felt when Jesus stopped and asked who touched Him? This was a crucial time for Jairus. His little daughter whom he loved was at the point of death; he had come to get Jesus to help and there was not much time. Jesus took the time to stop and see the woman who touched Him, who received healing from touching His hem, and told her that her faith had made her whole. Faith cometh by hearing and hearing by the Word of God.

But then here comes the bearer of the bad news from Jairus' house telling him not to bother Jesus, that it was too late, Jairus' daughter was dead. Before Jairus has a chance to latch on to that negative report, the scripture says that as soon as Jesus heard the word, he told Jairus not to be afraid but to believe.

> *As soon as Jesus heard the word that was spoken, he saith unto the ruler of the synagogue, Be not afraid, only believe.*
>
> —Mark 5: 36

Jairus had just minutes before witnessed the healing of the woman with the issue of blood and had heard Jesus tell her that her faith had made her whole. Jairus had heard the report from man but he received the words of Jesus in faith. Faith cometh by hearing and hearing by the Word of God.

Jairus received, believed and obeyed the Word of the Lord! The Word of God is the final authority!

When Jesus restored sight to the two blind men, the Word was received in faith.

> *And when he was come into the house, the blind men came to him: and Jesus saith unto them, Believe ye that I am able to do this? They said unto him, Yea, Lord. Then touched he their eyes, saying, According to your faith be it unto you.*
>
> —Matt. 9:28

The people brought a man sick of palsy to Jesus and let him down through the roof because of the crowd.

Jesus could see their faith. The evidence of their faith was their actions!

> *When Jesus saw their faith, he said unto the sick of the palsy, Son, thy sins be forgiven thee.*
> —Mark 2:5

When God commanded Elijah to go by the brook Cherith and the ravens would feed him, Elijah moved in faith. By faith, he made himself available to receive from the Lord, and the Word mixed with faith, profited Elijah! Because Elijah was available to the Word, received the Word, believed the Word, and obeyed the Word the miracle took place!

> *And the word of the LORD came unto him, saying, Get thee hence, and turn thee eastward, and hide thyself by the brook Cherith, that is before Jordan. And it shall be, that thou shalt drink of the brook; and I have commanded the ravens to feed thee there. So he went and did according unto the word of the LORD: for he went and dwelt by the brook Cherith, that is before Jordan. And the ravens brought him bread and flesh in the morning, and bread and flesh in the evening; and he drank of the brook.*
> —1 Kings 17:2-6

Believing has to do directly with the Word. Believing God has to do with what He has spoken. God spoke the Word and He was made flesh. How can we resist Him and be believers. And if the Word is what is spoken by

God, how can we not recognize the Word of God as the Son of God which comes out from God and was made flesh.

The Word of God shall always be and shall define, categorize and declare everything to be anything that it shall be. The Word of God is therefore to be greatly feared and greatly respected. Whether we internalize the Word as *it* or *Him,* we recognize that He is greatly to be feared and that He is high and lifted up and we are low and small and weak and needy. The living, powerful, awesome expression of the Father—that's who Jesus is. That's what the Word is.

Availability through faith

So we see that availability through faith makes us open to the Word.

If one would seek to be receptive of knowledge from the Word of God, he or she must do the work prerequisite.

> *And ye shall seek me, and find me, when ye shall search for me with all your heart.*
>
> —Jer. 29:13

The work of the seeker is to be available to the Word. This done, we are born again. It is faith that caused us to seek and be available, so we are born by the Word through faith. The light shineth in the darkness by the command of God and the darkness comprehended it not. The Word is born into our flesh but our flesh did not overcome it. The Word is the Light; the Light is the life that shines unto all men that they might know the love of God. But when the Light came unto the light, the light received not the Light as the owner-creator of the light.

Of his own will begat he us with the word of truth, that we should be a kind of firstfruits of his creatures.
—John 1:4-5

In him was life; and the life was the light of men.
—James 1:18

And the light shineth in darkness; and the darkness comprehended it not.

That was the true Light, which lighteth every man that cometh into the world. He was in the world, and the world was made by him, and the world knew him not. He came unto his own, and his own received him not.

—John 1:9-11

For God, who commanded the light to shine out of darkness, hath shined in our hearts, to give the light of the knowledge of the glory of God in the face of Jesus Christ.

—2 Cor. 4:6

*This then is the message which we have heard of him,
and declare unto you, that God is light, and in him is
no darkness at all.*

—1 John 1:5

*Then spake Jesus again unto them, saying, I am the
light of the world: he that followeth me shall not walk
in darkness, but shall have the light of life.*

—John 8:12

*Ye are the light of the world. A city that is set on an
hill cannot be hid.*

—Matt. 5:14-16

Neither do men light a candle, and put it under a
bushel, but on a candlestick; and it giveth light unto
all that are in the house. Let your light so shine before
men, that they may see your good works, and glorify
your Father which is in heaven.

What Is Faith?

FAITH

Faith is simply, "**I BELIEVE GOD**" Romans 4:3
says, *"For what saith the scripture? Abraham believed God,
and it was counted unto him for righteousness."*

Abraham believed God. He believed that what God
said was true. That's faith. He didn't try to analyze it
and he didn't try to dissect it. He received God's Word
because God said it. God has made it very simple for

us. Faith is that we believe Him. It is not a complicated thing, but spiritual. If you are too wise in your own eyes, you won't be able to just believe God. You will always try to figure Him out with your own mind, instead of having the mind of Christ.

> O the depth of the riches both of the wisdom and knowledge of God! how unsearchable are his judgments, and his ways past finding out!
>
> —Rom. 11:33

Allow us to stop for a moment and talk a little about faith.

The presuppositions of any stated rendering ultimately brings it back to the realm of faith, unless it purports like the big bang to be the very true beginning of physical reality, in which case there is a non-evidenced faith requirement within the postulate that far exceeds faith in God.

The foundation on which any statement is made is normally not elemental enough to be without a need for faith to accept its incipient concept. The realm of faith is required for any postulate. If you are saying that something is true, you must ultimately go back to faith to say it. The elements in the statement have to each be proved if it is science and since one would have to return to the very creation of atomic elements and molecules in order to make a statement about the physical reality, one finds himself at loss to be scientific and must resort to the big bang or something equally preposterous in order to dignify the foundation of any statement.

Since faith is necessary for any truth, there is not a reasonable need for truth to be known by science. Because science cannot prove the fundamental elements and how they came into being, they have to ultimately start with "I believe," and that's faith. So ultimately they would have to start out with a faith presupposition. It's not a proven thing. You're going to have to believe something that you can't otherwise prove. You cannot prove anything without faith. If my presupposition has faith in it and my first cause is God then that's where I will start, and I will say that everything I know, I know from God.

But if you start where you start from, can you show where your basis for thought and belief stem from?

The issue of how can we know, epistemology, comes into question. We can know by discovery or at least we think we can. But if I want to talk about total truth I have to talk about origins. And it's a very difficult thing....

If there was no intelligent creation but happenstance and accident, why does creation seem to have perfect design and why do humans believe in purpose and reasonability? Why are things so answerable one to another on the planet earth...just by accident or happenstance? Of course the question always is going to end up, Could there have been as easily something else as opposed to what is? Why... *if we're just an accident?*

We know that Jesus Christ is the Word of the Lord and we know that the prepositional statements given by the prophets is the Word of the Lord. We know that the Word of the Lord created all things and by Him all things consist, whether they be material or spiritual; all things were made by Him and for Him. We know that God has set His Word above all His name; it cannot fail. We know that God sent His Word and He said that it would not return to me void but that it would accomplish everything that He sent it out to do. We know therefore that the Word has work to do, therefore, we know that it cannot be a dead Word and we know that it can't be Word that has limits. It's God's Word and He has stated that it would not return to Him empty except that it has done what He told it to do.

We know that life comes from the Word for all men. Light comes and we know that the darkness is incapable of enveloping the light. The light shineth in the darkness and the darkness comprehended it not (enveloped, smothered, closed it in). The fact that the darkness could not comprehend it and enveloped it shows that the light is stronger than darkness. Wherever there is darkness, the light will cut right through it and be light. But the darkness cannot be darkness and enter the light; in order for the darkness to come into the light it must become light or simply cease. Even so the Word cannot be overcome by the lie, in the same way life cannot be overcome by death.

Again the Word of God is greater than the sum of its known parts. It continues to be effective and to grow and to change us well after the immediacy of its reception,

Now unto him that is able to do exceeding abundantly above all that we ask or think, according to the power that worketh in us,

—Ephe. 4:20 20

105

Everything that we receive has to do with the power that worketh within us. Because He lives, we are alive; because He authors our faith and our lives, our days and our years, we are always full of hope and encouragement. Even in dark days the Word will not die, the Christ will never die again; because His living Word is in us, we shall not die.

Have faith in God

And Jesus answering saith unto them, Have faith in God. For verily I say unto you, That whosoever shall say unto this mountain, Be thou removed, and be thou cast into the sea; and shall not doubt in his heart, but shall believe that those things which he saith shall come to pass; he shall have whatsoever he saith.

—Mark 11:22-24

As we have said previously, the only reason for us to believe anything is that God said it. If it originates in me I have reason to doubt it, but if God said it I have no reason to doubt it. I agree with God and say what He says, and then I shall have it. It is God, therefore, whom we are to believe. It is God who speaks reality. When we receive what He says, obey it, speak it, and believe it, then all that He says we shall have.

He sent his word and healed them and delivered them from their destructions.

—Ps. 107:20

So shall my word be that goeth forth out of my mouth: it shall not return unto me void, but it shall accomplish that which I please, and it shall prosper in the thing whereto I sent it.

—Isa. 55:11

My son, attend to my words; incline thine ear unto my sayings. Let them not depart from thine eyes; keep them in the midst of thine heart. For they are life unto those that find them, and health to all their flesh.

—Prov. 4:20-21

Jesus Christ is the Word and by His name many were healed. Because He is the Word, He accomplished the things that the Father sent Him to accomplish—healing, delivering, and restoring. As the Word, He healed, He taught, He delivered, He corrected, He died as the Word, and as the Word He could not stay dead but rose up accomplishing the will of the Father. He also expressed the Father by His life and deeds. The Word always demonstrated Himself in that it was impossible for Him to lie.

If we ask anything according to His will, it's going to happen; His Word and His will are synonymous. If we are going to speak according to His will we must know His Word and we must speak what He speaks if the things that we speak are to be true. Therefore we cannot have what we say, unless we say what He has spoken, unless we speak His Word, His will, His way.

Going back to the Word in Mark 11:22-24, we find speaking to the tree has to do with the first thing that

Jesus says, and that is what we must do, "Have faith in God." That's the first reference. Having faith in God means to believe God, and as it was with Abraham who was the father of the faith, it is also with us if we believe God; it is counted to us for righteousness. When we believe God, that is faith. Believing God presupposes that God has given us His Word and we have believed it. Therefore, if we would speak anything, God must have spoken it first. And if we believed it and spoke it also, in such case it shall come to pass.

Agree With What God Said

It's not so much what I speak, but what I agree with God in; that is what comes to pass. The Bible says out of the abundance of the heart, the mouth speaketh. My mouth does not originate anything anyway. God has to put it in my heart to speak. I trust that which God speaks to my heart. God speaks to us by revelation, and by His Spirit, by His present Spirit, He gives us illumination that works right now, individually with me, through me and sometimes even for me. You must receive the Word by faith, not by your comprehension of the Word.

You will not understand and then make a decision to receive the Word; you receive in faith by faith, then you will understand. You will not analyze and figure out the Word and then concur with God out of your mind. God does not want your concurrence. He does not want you to find Him to be correct and then concur with Him. He wants you to receive from Him and then walk in the things that He has said. God says, "Just trust me and receive what I have for you and then when you walk in it you'll find out its absolute truth."

AMEN! AMEN! AMEN! AMEN! AMEN!

I thank thee, O Father, Lord of heaven and earth, because thou hast hid these things from the wise and prudent, and hast revealed them unto babes.
—Matt. 11:25

Some are too wise and too proud to receive from God in faith!

Except you come to the Word with reverence, honor and faith as that which comes from God you may find only the general wisdom (which is still good) if you apply that Word by use of your own carnal mind. But if you receive the Word by faith, then it will supernaturally implement what you are and who you are.

If you prayerfully receive the Word, when you live and work and move in reality, whatever is placed in your Spirit, that which you have received by faith, will cause you to make a decision or do a thing differently than those around you. This will ultimately bring you to a different place and will bring glory to God. If others around you really believed that the Word was what God says it is they would be greedy for it and it would enter them as a living all-powerful personality and effect everything about them and their total reality. We're not talking about memorization; we are speaking of faith reception, not by just seeking to apply my mental capacities to the Word of God.

One has to actually believe that the Word of God will use me, not vice versa. The Word is the superior and I am the inferior so when I make myself available; that which is greater than I takes hold of me to use me.

Faith is Now

Now faith is the substance of things hoped for, the evidence of things not seen. Where is this substance and evidence to be experienced? Substance is that which occupies space and evidence is that which may be seen. *Therefore, the senses may experience each of these qualities. Where will the senses have contact with this substance and where will it observe this evidence?* The substance is found in the acts and behavior of the one hoping. And the things not seen shall be seen in the one also who is hoping or believing. Also by my actions and behaviors I show my faith. As James says that works show faith. Evidence – things seen. *Vid* means seen, *e* means out of, out of seeing. How can I see things that I can't see? It shows up in substance, in what I do. I bring forth substance because I hope and my behaviors cause it to come forth; the walk of faith brings forth the hope of the one believing.

The Book of James tells us, *"For as the body without the Spirit is dead, so faith without works is dead also."* We know that the body is alive because the breath, *pneuma,* the Spirit, breathes life into it. What we do is the evidence that there is faith. *If we have faith we will do.* Christ Jesus, is the author and finisher of our faith. We are following His course, the faith course, the walk of faith.

As Naaman dipped into the Jordan, his hope was to be healed from leprosy. He demonstrated his faith by obeying the word of the man of God and dipping in the Jordan seven times.

Then went he down, and dipped himself seven times in Jordan, according to the saying of the man of God: and his flesh came again like unto the flesh of a little child, and he was clean.
—2 Kings 5:14

Joshua believed God when God told him, "I have given into thine hand, Jericho…" So Joshua *did* as the Lord said and instructed the children of Israel to march around the city every day for six days and on the seventh day march around the city seven times, the priest blew the trumpet and all the people shouted and by faith the walls fell down.

By faith the walls of Jericho fell down, after they were compassed about seven days.
—Heb. 11:30

The Newborn Saint

Jesus told Nicodemus that he must be born again to see the kingdom of God. God's kingdom is in the spiritual realm. You cannot see God operating unless you have been born again. Then, and only then, can we see through God's eyes. Remember when we are born again, He has engrafted us in, allowing us to receive of Himself!

The newborn saint, born of the Word which is from above, now continues to maturity by making himself intentionally available to the Word through the hearing and reading of the Word in faith. The Word which is alive does its perfecting work in the saint according to the appointment of God.

For whom he did foreknow, he also did predestinate to be conformed to the image of his Son, that he might be the firstborn among many brethren.
—Rom. 8:29

Of his own will begat he us with the word of truth, that we should be a kind of firstfruits of his creatures.
—James 1:18

But as many as received him, to them gave he power to become the sons of God, even to them that believe on his name:
—John 1:12

Which were born, not of blood, nor of the will of the flesh, nor of the will of man, but of God.
—John 1:13

Being born again, not of corruptible seed, but of incorruptible, by the word of God, which liveth and abideth for ever.
—1 Pet. 1:23

We Must Believe the Word!

As newborn babes, desire the sincere milk of the word, that ye may grow thereby:

—1 Pet. 2:2

But he answered and said, It is written, Man shall not live by bread alone, but by every word that proceedeth out of the mouth of God.

—Matt. 4:4

CHAPTER 7

The Word Teaches

Just as a newborn baby is patiently taught by his mother, so the Word of God teaches the newborn saint, the Word baby. The Word of God teaches. It is a Spirit. I have not learned in the natural; I have not been taught in the natural. They happened in me somewhere beyond my reach. The Word, the living Word mixed with faith, grew and became and I was subject. God, by the revelation of His Word conceived understanding in me. I am not smart, I am not analytical, and I am not filled with residual empirical knowledge. I cannot manipulate even the illumination that God shines from me. I am humbled because it happens *through* me and not from me. I receive wisdom and understanding that is beyond me by the grace of God. It is a reception and not an obtaining or attaining. By this I mean it is a gift, not something that I can celebrate that I have done.

Communication and knowledge of God is known by and from the Spirit to the spirit. He imparts it. It is not because someone is smart enough to read it twenty times. If my congregation thinks that about me, then they are missing the miracle. The miracle is that even if I read it twenty times, in my own self I am not capable of remembering it. I have stood many times and looked out and said, "Help me, Jesus, what am I going to say to these your people this day? Lord help me; show me what to say. I'm not interested to delivering a well thought out outline. Lord, let me speak your Word to your people; let me be your vessel; reach down in me and use that which you have deposited in there. Use me, Lord. I don't know how to use me but you know how to use me. You deserve to use me. I don't know how to put it all together. I don't know what's in the hearts and minds of the people. All I can do is make myself available knowing that you put it there and you will pour it out. I don't want anyone to be impressed with me. I don't want to speak in such a way that everybody talks about how deep I am. Lord God, you are so sweet, I just want to be able to speak to your people."

I don't have anything unless He gives it to me. The Lord will give me what to say because He gave me the job. I don't come in here with intellect and smartness. I don't have to be smart. My job is to stay in the Word and pray and allow His Word to use me. Ask the Lord to use you and the Lord will use you if you have made yourself available to Him.

For who maketh thee to differ from another? and what hast thou that thou didst not receive? Now if thou didst receive it, why dost thou glory, as if thou hadst not received it?

—I Cor. 4:7

I don't brag on my education because my education is not the basis of my stance. The fact is, I stand because God blesses me. God has placed me here and wherever He places you He will be the one to give you the wisdom to carry out the work if you can put down what you think you have.

So either we receive what we have from God or it is not something that we are supposed to have. So if we received it, let us not be as Herod who refused to give glory unto God (Acts 12:21). If we have not received it, let us not be like the false prophets who speak out of their own minds (Jeremiah 23). But we must be humble, knowing that God has graced us with His treasures.

Now when they saw the boldness of Peter and John, and perceived that they were unlearned and ignorant men, they marveled; and they took knowledge of them, that they had been with Jesus.

—Acts 4:13

The Scripture reveals to us that Peter and John were unlearned and ignorant men. They were not haughty, but they were humbly available in faith, empowered by the Holy Ghost; they were vessels receiving the full flow of spiritual wisdom and revelational knowledge from God.

Read the Word in faith. People go to the Word and when they are finished they say they didn't get anything out of it, that they didn't understand it. They have the idea that they should be able to break it down right, analyze and hash it out. They think that what they know their brain can regurgitate as if the Word of God is a biology book.

Whatever you retain in your mind is not what you really received. What you really received was spiritual and it was delivered to the spiritual being that you are, not to your gray matter. There is much that you have that your gray matter doesn't even know that you have because you read and received God's Word. Now when God sends you to someone or sends someone to you, the Word starts rising up in you and you are able to speak boldly for God.

When God calls you to use what you have, God will bring it up. Peter and John had been with Jesus and were filled with the Word. The Lord used them to turn the whole world upside-down. Develop a new way of seeing what you have received, and know that God will use it when it's time. God does not use those who are in themselves wise by humanistic measure. You have to be willing to be used of God to speak things spiritually. Forget about yourself. God uses those who are base, lowly, and humble. He cannot use us if we are high-minded. We must get low.

For ye see your calling, brethren, how that not many wise men after the flesh, not many mighty, not many noble, are called: But God hath chosen the foolish things of the world to confound the wise; and God hath chosen the weak things of the world to confound the things which are mighty; And base things of the world, and things which are despised, hath God chosen, yea, and things which are not, to bring to nought things that are: That no flesh should glory in his presence.

—I Cor. 1:26-29

A person who has subjected himself under the Word has been with Jesus and there is revelation from the Word of God that makes a man able without benefit of letters to have knowledge of the deep things of God. *And God gets the glory!*

The Word which is Spirit teaches the Spirit man. This is pure knowledge, true knowledge, the only real knowledge. This is the knowledge and wisdom that keeps the newborn alive and causes it to grow and mature. When we come before the Word, we must be teachable. We must come before him praying, "Teach me Lord what you would have me to know."

For the Jews require a sign, and the Greeks seek after wisdom: But we preach Christ crucified, unto the Jews a stumblingblock, and unto the Greeks foolishness; But unto them which are called, both Jews and Greeks, Christ the power of God, and the wisdom of God. Because the foolishness of God is wiser than men; and the weakness of God is stronger than men.

—1 Cor. 1:18-29

God has delivered to you things that are too much for your brain and carnal mind to handle. God has given to us by His Spirit. He does not speak to our brain by His Spirit. He speaks to our spirit by His Spirit. Your mind cannot understand spiritual things; if you keep that Spirit man covered and continue to speak out of the brain-housing group, you will always speak carnally.

You have to know that God has been depositing into your Spirit-self things that your brain cannot comprehend. Quit checking with your brain to try to find out what you know.

> *But of him are ye in Christ Jesus, who of God is made unto us wisdom, and righteousness, and sanctification, and redemption: That, according as it is written, He that glorieth, let him glory in the Lord.*
>
> —1 Cor. 1:30-31

Remember Saul had much education and had been taught by the great teachers of his time.

> *I am verily a man which am a Jew, born in Tarsus, a city in Cilicia, yet brought up in this city at the feet of Gamaliel, and taught according to the perfect manner of the law of the father....*
>
> —Acts 22:3

Before Saul received the living Word of God, he persecuted Christians. After he met and submitted to Christ on the Damascus Road, he was changed and humbled. He became a receptor of spiritual revelation, setting man's wisdom aside and began teaching and preaching Jesus Christ crucified by the power and demonstration of the Holy Spirit. *To God be the glory!*

> *And I, brethren, when I came to you, came not with excellency of speech or of wisdom, declaring unto you the testimony of God. For I determined not to know any thing among you, save Jesus Christ, and him crucified. And I was with you in weakness, and in fear, and in much trembling. And my speech and my preaching was not with enticing words of man's wisdom, but in demonstration of the Spirit and of power: that your faith should not stand in the wisdom of men, but in the power of God.*
>
> —1 Cor. 2:1-4

We're not dealing with academics, but that which the Holy Ghost teacheth. We're not trying to look at spiritual things with carnal knowledge but comparing Spiritual with spiritual.

We believe that academic accomplishment capacity through empirical discovery is sensual and carnal. There is a difference between academics and revelation and we're claiming that the academic is sensual and carnal and must not be the means by which people of God receive the things of God.

It is not your capacity that you brought to the table. God will capacitate you. He will give you the capacity to do what He wants you to do. He will grow you. God is putting things in your Spirit man but if your brain is the ruler of the day, then you will not receive.

The things of God are spiritually discerned. Spiritual truth is not to be known through human wisdom.

But as it is written, Eye hath not seen, nor ear heard, neither have entered into the heart of man, the things which God hath prepared for them that love him. But God hath revealed them unto us by his Spirit: for the Spirit searcheth all things, yea, the deep things of God. For what man knoweth the things of a man, save the spirit of man which is in him? even so the things of God knoweth no man, but the Spirit of God. Now we have received, not the spirit of the world, but the Spirit which is of God; that we might know the things that are freely given to us of God. Which things also we speak, not in the words which man's wisdom teacheth, but which the Holy Ghost teacheth; comparing spiritual things with spiritual. But the natural man receiveth not the things of the Spirit of God: for they are foolishness unto him: neither can he know them, because they are spiritually discerned.

—1 Cor. 2:9

God makes known His Word to us by revelation.

Turn you at my reproof: behold, I will pour out my Spirit unto you, I will make known my words unto you.
—Prov. 1:23

It is a parallel. Each of the things spoken is equal to the other in perfect mutual equality. So it is that making

His Word known to us is equal to Him pouring out His Spirit unto us. Let us understand again that God's Word is God's Spirit and God's Spirit is God's Word. So we can understand why the Word is called the living and powerful and how it is that it can be a discerner of the deep things of our physicality and our spirit.

As the Word of God teaches us, we begin to grow. The Word of God empowers us to become the sons of God.

Only as Much as the Vessel Has Been Hollowed Out Can It Be Filled

That I may know him, and the power of his resurrection, and the fellowship of his sufferings, being made conformable unto his death;

—Phili. 3:10

Heaven and earth shall pass away, but my words shall not pass away.

—Matt. 24: 35

If the pains and sorrows of this life have really carved out the vessel, it can hold more. I don't believe that we will all be able to enjoy Him on the same level because suffering is the primary thing that makes a vessel able to appreciate God and be filled with Him.

The more you can be filled with God the more you can enjoy Him. The greatest bliss in all reality is the capacity to enjoy God.

The more that we are Word, the more we share in His divinity.

> *Grace and peace be multiplied unto you through the knowledge of God, and of Jesus our Lord, According as his divine power hath given unto us all things that pertain unto life and godliness, through the knowledge of him that hath called us to glory and virtue: Whereby are given unto us exceeding great and precious promises: that by these ye might be partakers of the divine nature, having escaped the corruption that is in the world through lust.*
>
> —2 Pet. 1:2-4

We may be able to grow here on earth faster than we could in eternity because there's more adversity, suffering and pain that we must confront. I believe to some degree that does have to do with the building and gaining and growth that the new creature has.

The Demonstration of the Holy Spirit

> *And I, brethren, when I came to you, came not with excellency of speech or of wisdom, declaring unto you the testimony of God. For I determined not to know any thing among you, save Jesus Christ, and him crucified. And I was with you in weakness, and in fear, and in much trembling. And my speech and my preaching was not with enticing, words of man's wisdom, but in demonstration of the Spirit and of power: that your*

faith should not stand in the wisdom of men, but in the power of God.

—2 Cor. 2:4

When the Word is preached, something supernatural occurs. Something takes place beyond that which our eyes are able to see, ears are able to hear, nor our minds able to conceive. It is spiritual. The Holy Spirit demonstrates the Word, because the Word of God is life-power. The Word of God expresses Himself to those who are Spirit born. The essence of what takes place cannot be captured on tape, audio or visual.

The things of God are spiritually discerned, meaning, they are only understood by a spiritual being. The brute beast will not and cannot assess spiritual rendering. Those things that the ear can hear and the eye can see are merely carriers of unseen power and authority and the transmission and the reception is threshed and the produce is separated from the residual physical and the seen elements.

When we are preaching, you see the vessel and you hear the words; they carry the power of God and these things are transferred to the spiritual being waiting for reception. And so, communication, transmission and reception are completed. And by this means, the Holy Spirit demonstrates His capacity for communication of doctrine. In other words, when we are doing what we do, everybody in the room can hear something and see something, whether they be spiritual or carnal, but they that are spiritual have also ears to hear, eyes to see, what the Holy Spirit reveals.

You may even explain the Word and not understand the Word. On some level you have spiritually received in your spirit knowledge from God's Word, but your brain has not yet been made a participant and therefore on some human level it has not been open for you to know what you know in the Spirit. But when the Lord calls you to speak it, He operates through your brain so that your mouth may speak. At that point your brain becomes a participant to some degree in the things of God and the Spirit.

> *It is the Spirit that quickeneth; the flesh profiteth nothing: the words that I speak unto you, they are Spirit, and they are life.*
>
> —John 6:63

Our faith stands by revelation of the Spirit of God and not by the wisdom of man.

> *But as it is written, Eye hath not seen, nor ear heard, neither have entered into the heart of man, the things which God hath prepared for them that love him.*
> *But God hath revealed them unto us by his Spirit: for the Spirit searcheth all things, yea, the deep things of God. For what man knoweth the things of a man, save the spirit of man which is in him? even so the things of God knoweth no man, but the Spirit of God.*
> *Now we have received, not the spirit of the world, but the Spirit which is of God; that we might know the things that are freely given to us of God. Which things*

also we speak, not in the words which man's wisdom teacheth, but which the Holy Ghost teacheth; comparing spiritual things with spiritual. But the natural man receiveth not the things of the Spirit of God: for they are foolishness unto him: neither can he know them, because they are spiritually discerned. But he that is spiritual judgeth all things, yet he himself is judged of no man. or who hath known the mind of the Lord, that he may instruct him? But we have the mind of Christ.

—1 Cor. 2:9-16

We have the mind of Christ?

Yes, we believe that the Word of God is the content and structure, the author and the builder of the mind of Christ in us.

For He said that as many as received Him (He is the Word of God) to them gave He *power* to become the sons of God. We know that there is *power* in the name of Christ and the Word of God. He, the Word of God, is alive and *powerful* (Hebrews 4:12) and knows our thoughts and intents. He is the communicated will and the faith, authored and finished by Himself, who is also called the Word of God.

For my thoughts are not your thoughts, neither are your ways my ways, saith the LORD. For as the heavens are higher than the earth, so are my ways higher than your ways, and my thoughts than your thoughts.

—Isa. 55:8-9

To have the mind of Christ is to think like Christ and to know His will. His will is His Word. His Word is His expression. We know that the Scripture tells us that His ways and thoughts are higher than ours. Our minds must be renewed. By receiving the Word of God, we renew our minds. If I am thinking in the flesh in some areas of my life then those are the areas that my mind is in need of renewing. Our minds must be reconstructed by the Word of God.

> *It is the Spirit that quickeneth; the flesh profiteth nothing: the words that I speak unto you, they are spirit, and they are life.*
>
> —John 6:63

The Bible says the Spirit quickeneth, which means the Spirit makes us live. The Words of God can make you live because they are Spirit and they are life. Matthew 4:4:1 *"But he answered and said, 'It is written, Man shall not live by bread alone, but by every word that proceedeth out of the mouth of God.'"*

The Word is Spirit and gives us birth and life, hence spiritual life, hence divine life.

Though the doctor may be able to look at you and understand that through the life processes it is time you will die, but the life will continue as long as the Spirit says *"live!"* The flesh does not decide how long the being lives, but the Spirit decides.

> *I am crucified with Christ: nevertheless I live; yet not I, but Christ liveth in me: and the life which I now live*

*in the flesh I live by the faith of the Son of God, who
loved me, and gave himself for me.*

—Gal. 2:20

*For ye are dead, and your life is hid with Christ in
God.*

—Col. 3:3

We have the divine nature.

—I Pet. 5:4

The Word of God as a Language – The Language of Truth. Speak to me Lord!

The Word of God is the means of spiritual, heavenly
communication. It is not merely the message but also
the means of spiritual speech by which the Lord speaks
specific information to the believer. The Word, having
been received and believed, is the definer, illustrator, and
interpreter of truth and reality. And furthermore the
Word brings the contrast to all we know so that we can
have differentiation of what we understand and perceive
in the world. The problem that we have in receiving the
benefit of the language is unbelief because the Lord has
informed us that the Word is alive and powerful and that
it is a discerner of the deep things physical and spiritual.
Having this Word then in us, we are enabled to see and
to understand the reality around us. We are able also
to receive from the Lord those things that we need to
know in our individual lives as His children and as servants of His. But except that we believe that His Word

can speak to us to teach us and direct us to inform us and to guide us, we miss the benefit because we believe that its for our carnal brain and merely something to be remembered.

It is important for us to realize that the Word is alive and as such it grows, it reproduces, it expands. The Word is somewhat like an antenna; by it God can target us and speak to us in that we have receptive capability. God directs us, guides us, leads us, and helps us to make the decisions and choices in our lives by His Word. The Word is able to speak to any area of our lives.

The Word is a language. When saints are communicating with each other there are things that are awakened that may not have been spoken. There is a spiritual knowing

When the Holy Spirit comes, God enables us to speak with new tongues. The heavenly language comes by means of that which is in the Spirit man, which is the Word of God, and is the means for communication between saint and saint, saint and God. There is no communication that disagrees in any language except the lie. So by putting the Word in us we prepare ourselves for the benefits of being children of God and saints of God. We are enabled thereby to receive commandment and to be good servants of God.

Our communication is supernatural. It's not carnal; it's not a product of the flesh, but of the Spirit, and that which is born of the Spirit is spirit so says our Lord Jesus Christ as He spoke to Nicodemus.

He has given us the power to become the sons of God. The Word received mixed with faith births us and as we receive more of His Word, the more we grow and mature into the sons of God.

> *But as it is written, Eye hath not seen, nor ear heard, neither have entered into the heart of man, the things which God hath prepared for them that love him.*
>
> *But God hath revealed them unto us by his Spirit: for the Spirit searcheth all things, yea, the deep things of God. For what man knoweth the things of a man, save the Spirit of man which is in him? even so the things of God knoweth no man, but the Spirit of God.*
>
> *Now we have received, not the spirit of the world, but the Spirit which is of God; that we might know the things that are freely given to us of God. Which things also we speak, not in the words which man's wisdom teacheth, but which the Holy Ghost teacheth; comparing spiritual things with spiritual. But the natural man receiveth not the things of the Spirit of God: for they are foolishness unto him: neither can he know them, because they are spiritually discerned. But he that is spiritual judgeth all things, yet he himself is judged of no man. For who hath known the mind of the Lord, that he may instruct him? But we have the mind of Christ.*
>
> —1 Cor. 2:9-16

He can speak to me; he can tell me things that I didn't know before, future things. The Word talks to us; by the Word of God you know where things are going. He knows the thoughts and intents of our hearts. It is as plain a statement that you'll find anywhere in the Word about this word. And to think of the Word as a knower, a discerner, to break it down and differentiate its capacities. It knows me; it knows the depth of my being. It's capable of changing me and making me powerful enough to do things for God.

The Word of God is powerful. We have to get to the point where we really comprehend. There are angels here but we can't get to them without the Word. We wouldn't know they were here without the Word. The Word is capable of being our friend and walking with us. He is the Holy Spirit. It's Him; it's Himself; it's the only thing that we really have here. Everything else we know fails us, everything! Everything else changes, but the Word is true.

From Glory to Glory

> *But we all, with open face beholding as in a glass the glory of the Lord, are changed into the same image from glory to glory, even as by the Spirit of the Lord.*
>
> —2 Cor. 3:18

His Word changes us. Being changed from glory to glory, beholding truth as in a mirror. His Word is truth. When He speaks to us and we obey, we are changed. If we look at something that is beautiful long enough we desire to be beautiful in the same way. Face to face with truth, we must change. We change by beholding Him. The Word shows us who He is and shows us who we are. As a sculptor looks upon his sculpting and whittles away at the unformed material, making it into what he intended for it to be, the Word is able to cut away those things that are unlike Him, changing us from glory to glory.

> *For the Word of God is quick, and powerful, and sharper than any twoedged sword, piercing even to the dividing asunder of soul and spirit, and of the joints and marrow, and is a discerner of the thoughts and intents of the heart. Neither is there any creature that is not manifest in his sight: but all things are naked and opened unto the eyes of him with whom we have to do.*
>
> —Heb. 4:12

He sees through us; we are naked and open to Him. We cannot hide from God. When God asked Adam in the garden, "Where art thou?" it was not because He did not know where Adam was. When He asked Cain, "Where is your brother Abel?" it was not because He did not know.

Are you really willing to receive what the Lord is showing you about yourself? Will you come honestly before Him so that He can speak to you about you? Most times we deflect the truth about ourselves when the Word of God exposes us, therefore we do not confess. However, this is the work that we must first do before we can be effective in serving others. If we will receive His Word, we will be changed from glory to glory!

CHAPTER 8

And We Ask As Gideon Asked, Where Are The Miracles?

M iracles are based on faith. A faith community has to be built in order to have an environment for miracles to take place. What Jesus was doing was demonstrating that He would not do mighty works where there is no faith. The church was Jesus' planned environment for miracles. It is the responsibility of believers to gather together (church) in order to be unified as one body and by faith in revelation do the will of the head, which at times will be impossible, yet the church shall prevail. The living Word is and always will be the data for faith and the raw energy for power in the church. Faith makes use of the invisible, and readily performs the impossible, simply because the church believes what God has said without need of evidence or substance to indicate to the flesh that truth is present and available.

Community is defined as many in one. Co-unity together or together in unity. Many believers equal many members and one body. Unity, corporate, body—these are all the same essence, synonymous; one faith, one Spirit one baptism (1 Corinthians 12).

> *For God commanded the light to shine out of darkness hath shined in our hearts to give the light of knowledge of the glory of God in the face of Jesus Christ.*
> —2 Cor. 4:6

What if we actually became an environment of faith? What if we really decided to believe God? People could walk through the door of the church and get healed. Some of the churches in the book of Revelation were communities of faith; they were doing great things for the Lord but that didn't mean they didn't have any problems. Doing what pleases Jesus is what counts. If I am not doing what He wants me to do it doesn't count. What counts is if I really have a heart to do what He wants me to do and not what I want to do. Instead, we tell God what we want to do for Him.

The example of the community of believers in the book of Acts and how they love each other and forgive each other is the only way to get over stuff.

In the book of Acts, the people feared Peter because of his office. No man dared join themselves to their number. They did not compare or try to show their superiority.

In Acts, you notice that every time God showed Himself, what He did increased the fear.

And We Ask As Gideon Asked, Where Are The Miracles?

Now as soon as it was day, there was no small stir among the soldiers, what was become of Peter. And when Herod had sought for him, and found him not, he examined the keepers, and commanded that they should be put to death. And he went down from Judaea to Caesarea, and there abode. And Herod was highly displeased with them of Tyre and Sidon: but they came with one accord to him, and, having made Blastus the king's chamberlain their friend, desired peace; because their country was nourished by the king's country. And upon a set day Herod, arrayed in royal apparel, sat upon his throne, and made an oration unto them. And the people gave a shout, saying, It is the voice of a god, and not of a man. And immediately the angel of the Lord smote him, because he gave not God the glory: and he was eaten of worms, and gave up the ghost. But the word of God grew and multiplied. And the miracles increased.

—Acts 12:18

Whenever God showed Himself, the number of people who were saved increased. The apostles were not taken lightly and miracles increased because of the fear. Their salvation was not taken lightly. When the rulers of the people and elders of Israel saw the boldness of Peter and John and knew that they were unlearned men, they knew Peter and John had been with Jesus (Acts 4:13).

After Ananias and Sapphira were killed for lying to the Holy Ghost, the people's faith grew strong because the people feared God (Acts 5).

There should be a fear of God and an honor to the leaders of God. Then there will be growth.

People complain and find fault with leadership, not even knowing that Satan is using them, then Satan brings division.

God then must intervene and after He shows Himself, there is fear, honor, and then respect.

There have been faith communities that have existed for periods of time, but Satan has destroyed them while he works through the pride side of even so-called Christians. Satan is able to get a hold on people at the point of lust, covetousness, envy, jealousy, and out of these comes bitterness, division, anger, wrath, dissension, the spirit of comparison, which brings an attitude of inferiority or superiority in those who employ it.

So long as people have a focus on pleasing the Master, even to their own hurt, the community is enabled and faith deeds will prosper. It is the loss of focus where people look at themselves as it relates to lust and benefits that the evil spirit of division comes to fruition.

A community that is growing by and through the Word of God is so centered and focused on the Master that they are able to put away childish things. For the Word is that perfect thing that relegates imperfection to nothingness. As the perfection comes to us through the Word those things dissipate and are not needed and we put them away from us. It is imperfect for instance when the Word comes into me and says to me, *"Thou shalt not covet,"* and I am honest to say that I am coveting. That's when the Word is doing what it does; it changes me and when I am convicted by the Spirit (the Word), I confess that and the Lord changes me when I am honest. So by that means, the Word comes and does the perfect work and changes me upward into being like Jesus Christ.

The community of saints who are empowered as one body to do the greater things that Jesus spoke of and to do those things that He did shall move like a rushing river against the gates of hell. The gates shall not prevail; the gates will not be able to hold the prisoners in bondage, but the gates shall fall, the prisoners shall be released. Darkness shall flee and they shall bathe in the light of His glory. It is the thing that Jesus said: this day the scripture concerning those who sat in darkness and those who are released to light, this day the Scripture is fulfilled in their ears.

We are the continuation of his body to be the vessels used by God for prisoners to be set free and for those who sat in darkness to see great light. As a community we are the body of Christ, a corporate unified individual, capable of great things in Christ Jesus. We are moving up to higher ground without the schisms and division in the body. We must resist all of those things that would come to divide us and earnestly contend for the faith once delivered to the saints. We have to realize that unified we are an impregnable entity and an unstoppable force. We are the body of Christ!

God also works miracles through grace without the involvement of man's mind. A mind of faith is required to see or to discern the presence of the miraculous. So in order that the mind be capable, a new birth and a new mind must be in the person who would see spiritual things.

Unregenerate man sees the power of God after it's too late to repent. Thousands of men saw the power of God in the flood. In the judgment down through the Bible age, unregenerate men have seen the power of God mostly when it was too late. And they shall see it in the clouds when Christ returns and they are pining in sorrow.

God still works miracles where there are those who make themselves humbly available in faith. He has not changed. In Him there is neither variableness nor shadow of turning. "Jesus Christ, the same, yesterday, today and for ever."

The question is, do we really love the Lord enough, do we love His people enough to submit to His Word, and deny ourselves so that the church can increase! Are we really His servants, submitted to Him, or are we walking in the light of our own minds, serving ourselves, our own pleasures, motivated by our own pride and haughtiness?

If we would really become that environment, if we would really become subject to the Word, let it tell us what to do and how to do it, let it convict us, and clean us, and empower us, we could become that faith environment, receiving the unhindered flow of revelational knowledge from the mighty Word of God!

The church would be restored, lives would be changed, jail cells and hospital rooms would be emptied, the house of God would overflow with saints, there would be no lack, love would flow from breast to breast. We would again become that mighty bride of Christ walking in the power and might of God!

CHAPTER 9

*We Need God—
God Is Our
Source- He Is
Our All In All*

> *I am the vine, ye are the branches: He that abideth in me, and I in him, the same bringeth forth much fruit: for without me ye can do nothing.*
>
> —John 15:5

Without God we can do nothing.

> *God hath spoken once; twice have I heard this; that power belongeth unto God.*
>
> —Ps. 62:11

Why do we need God? We need the Word of Truth. We need God's revelational knowledge in order to know reality.

Do we need to know reality? That depends on whether we want to live simply in our carnality and die as does a worm or a hog. Or are we of a higher nature, desiring eternal life and joy?

Without God we cannot know the simplest things about this life that we are in. There are many who pursue the things of this life and attach themselves but they are not the peculiar people and they attach themselves to the things of this life. Deceived into thinking that they are living, they are actually dying a slow death.

The absolutes of truth and knowledge—so we cannot be sure of anything until our hearts are informed by undeniable truth itself. Source has everything to do with whether knowledge is knowledge.

We need God because we need to find the sources and the goals of our selves in this unknown reality. In short, if we are ever to know God, we need God to tell us the way and the destination. We need God to tell us who or what God is. We need God for God and without God we shall never be sure of God. If God does not disclose Himself we shall never know God.

You can live an entire life and never know God and never know that there is any need to know Him. God tells us that we need to know Him. God demonstrates that we are complete knowing Him and incomplete not knowing Him.

Having heard, we have faith to be available. Hearing comes by faith. Hearing is a predisposition of the heart and mind to receive from the Lord.

And ye shall seek me, and find me, when ye shall search for me with all your heart.

—Jer. 29:13

We Need God—God Is Our Source-
He Is Our All In All

One can seek God with his whole heart only because God has already found him. God has already performed His divine handiwork about which we have no knowledge but that our hearts are somehow affected. As Paul has said, "It is not in our flesh to do any good thing" and all that is good in us comes from God.

Yes, we need God. Just as a baby comes into the world crying out, needing warmth and love, needing its mother to nourish and feed it, we need God. A baby does not know exactly what it needs, but he is needy. We are born with that part of us that reaches out to something. That something is God. We sometimes go through most of our lives not realizing or submitting to that which we need. We try to fill it with other things, but they do not suffice. We need God. When we come to the place where we realize we need God and accept Jesus as Savior, we are born again. We are new babies, Word babies; our new life begins. We begin to grow by the Word of God. When the Word of God enters into us it grows within us and causes us to conform to the Word to become more like Jesus. The more the flow is unhindered, the more knowledge we receive, the faster we grow.

Of his own will begat he us with the word of truth, that we should be a kind of firstfruits of his creatures.
— James 1:18

But as many as received him, to them gave he power to become the sons of God, even to them that believe on his name:
— John 1:12

Which were born, not of blood, nor of the will of the flesh, nor of the will of man, but of God.

—John 1:13

Being born again, not of corruptible seed, but of incorruptible, by the word of God, which liveth and abideth for ever.

—1 Pet. 1:23

As newborn babes, desire the sincere milk of the word, that ye may grow thereby:

—1 Pet. 2:2

But he answered and said, It is written, Man shall not live by bread alone, but by every word that proceedeth out of the mouth of God.

—Matt. 4:4

When we see the little birds in their nest waiting patiently, expectantly for the mother bird to bring food, their eyes sometimes have not even opened yet and they cannot see, but in faith, their mouths are stretched wide open intentionally available to receive all that she has for them, and in time they will grow and become able to soar. We must be as trusting as those baby birds, coming before the Lord, humble hearts open, in faith, as little children, expecting to receive. Don't be so bright; just sit there with your little mouths open and the Holy Spirit will by the Word feed you. When you look at those little birds in the nest just say, That's me, I'm one of them, a little one who can't fly and go get anything to eat by himself. He's in the nest and he doesn't have his head down; his head is up and mouth open. But he's in that nest waiting on his feeding. We have to stay that way when God has brought us a great way in maturity. Don't ever get so smart that you don't have your mouth open. Don't be a know-it-all.

Get yourself fed. Make yourselves intentionally available to receive from Him. God promised if we believe Him and approach Him expectantly in faith then He would feed us. Believe Him; sit there and get your feeding in faith. Don't analyze it, be still trusting God, be available, open your mouth and be fed. If something is said that's amiss it won't even get to your mouth.

Preachers, do your job as oracles of God. Believe God. Do not be high-minded; humble yourselves. Be available. If you know everything, shut your mind down from what it thinks it knows. God will teach you things that you could have gone to school for twenty years and you never would be able to receive.

If you don't love His Word, you will believe a lie. It is of utmost importance. If you love it, you'll marry it, you'll be true to it, and you will receive it. Unless you receive it like a baby, you can't get it. You've got to believe it just because He said it.

Humble yourselves, be as a child, believe God, pray, ask God to feed you. God will do exactly what He said He would do. And, we would grow and become the powerful church that we have seen in the book of Acts. We would walk in the power of the God!

No, God has not changed; we have changed. Let us repent and humble ourselves in faith, and position ourselves to become all that God has called the church to be.

But as it is written, Eye hath not seen, nor ear heard, neither have entered into the heart of man, the things which God hath prepared for them that love him. But God hath revealed them unto us by his Spirit: for the Spirit searcheth all things, yea, the deep things of God. For what man knoweth the things of a man, save the spirit of man which is in him? even so the things of God knoweth no man, but the Spirit of God. Now we have received, not the spirit of the world, but the Spirit which is of God; that we might know the things that are freely given to us of God. Which things also we speak, not in the words which man's wisdom teacheth, but which the Holy Ghost teacheth; comparing spiritual things with spiritual. But the natural man receiveth not the things of the Spirit of God: for they are foolishness unto him: neither can he know them, because they are spiritually discerned.

—I Cor. 2:9-14

HO, EVERY ONE THAT THIRSTETH, COME YE TO THE WATERS....

—Isa. 55:1

And receive

THE UNHINDERED FLOW OF REVELATIONAL KNOWLEDGE FROM THE MIGHTY WORD OF GOD

HALLELUJAH! HALLELUJAH! HALLELUJAH!

PART II

RECEPTIONS FROM: THE UNHINDERED FLOW OF THE WORD OF GOD

The following are a series of knowledge receptions that we have included in this book, revealed by the living Word of God. These receptions have come to us as gifts of God because we have humbly and fearfully made ourselves available to the Word of God in order to receive the full flow of spiritual knowledge.

Our Revelational Knowledge Institute is a systematic intentional cooperation of souls bound in faith and submission to Jesus Christ gathered with expectation of illumination from the Word of God. Wonderful illumination has been forthcoming, as we have humbly made ourselves available by faith to the Word of God.

We have a response of grateful praise and not celebration of our capacity to obtain. We have received by grace and not by submitting the Word to our academic or scholastic aptitude. This series of receptions that has flowed unto us is identical with all revelation that is true.

Our prayer is that if you have not done so, you will also go before the Lord, humbly and in faith, and that when the Lord of Glory knocks, you will submit to Him, open the door and allow Him entrance into your heart.

Ho, every one that thirsteth, come ye to the waters....
—Isa. 55:1

And receive

THE UNHINDERED FLOW OF REVELATIONAL KNOWLEDGE FROM THE MIGHTY WORD OF GOD

The Unhindered Flow

According to 1 John 5:7-8, the water, the blood and the Spirit are in behavioral agreement. They all characteristically have a downward flow. Humility therefore is *the necessity* for an uninterrupted flow of Holy Spirit communication.

Where is the power and where are the miracles? Inquiring souls want to know! This book is the answer for those sensitive enough to know that the mighty flow, as related in the book of Acts, of knowledge and power from the Holy Spirit has been stemmed; the flow has ebbed.

A BOOK OF RECEPTIONS

(A reception is a revelation or an illumination beyond the sum of the syllabic word content received from the living Word of God to the soul that is humble, fearful and available in its regard to the written Word of God. These

three attitudes are absolute prerequisites to access the con-
tinuous flow of illumination and revelation that issues from
the Word of God.)

WHAT HAPPENED TO THE
APOSTOLIC POWER?

The church, though they be saints, are not receiving the full flow from God. *To approach His Word is
to approach Himself.* Academically we (humanity) approach Him (His Word) with the attitude that by shear
concentration of mind in analytical dissection we can
reduce the infinite Word of God to its simplest form
and consume it in finite-sized pieces, and by so doing,
comprehend God. What an insult to Almighty God!
What high-stepping humanity! It is no wonder that God
resists our prideful, intellectual forays.

Our attempts to pillage the Word of God rather than
to bow down and plead at His feet, is not only regret-
table, but dangerous. For God Himself reminds us that
He is a consuming fire!

Because today's church is comparatively weak and
because the miracles that were known in the book of Acts
and the epistles are not prevalent, we must join Gideon
in asking, "Where are the miracles?"

We know that we must be doing something wrong
because God does not change, for the Bible says: *"In
Him there is no variableness nor shadow of turning. Jesus
Christ, the same, yesterday, today and forever."* We must
admit that failure is not in God, but in humanity.

Summary

When we ask the Word of God, the Word makes our error clear. We have forgotten that God identifies with His Word. His Word must be respected; we must humble ourselves as we approach the Word and recognize that He (the Word) is alive as is stated in Hebrews 4:11-12 and that He is powerful. We must therefore be fearful in our approach to the Word of God. The Bible says, *"God resists the proud and gives grace to the humble."*

This book is greatly needed as a revelational source of information. It will be an inspiration to teachers and pastors. It will provide empowerment to workers for Christ who believe in the power of the Word of God and desire to see the demonstration of the Word in the church. They recognize a constricted flow of Holy Ghost power in their churches. Church members will benefit from this book who themselves are perplexed by the powerful promises of the true God who cannot lie nor fail, and yet the promises are not demonstrated in His beloved church.

It is our justification for writing a book, having an institute that is not humanistically grounded. Spiritual truth is not to be known through human wisdom.

There is therefore now no condemnation for those who walk in the Spirit. For they that are after the flesh do mind the things of the flesh; but they that are after the Spirit the things of the Spirit. For to be carnally minded is death; but to be spiritually minded is life and peace.

—Rom. 8:5-8

151

Because the carnal mind is enmity against God: for it is not subject to the law of God, neither indeed can be. So then they that are in the flesh cannot please God.

As a race coming to birth through Christ Jesus, there is not just a specific few to know God, but He has now made a way thru the second Adam that they may receive spiritual knowledge. Being born again of the Spirit now they can receive from the spiritual Word and presence of God. They can receive, whereas when they were totally carnal they were unable to receive. So they had to be born again because their carnal minds could not receive the things of God.

They that are after the flesh do mind the things of the flesh, but they that are after the Spirit mind the things after the Spirit.

If we try to confuse spiritual things with carnal things then it must be that our quest is carnal. If we try to be double minded then we will have darkness. But we cannot, as we seek the things of God, do it on a carnal or humanistic framework or if we seek kudos from humans we will be blinded and will not know and see what God wants us to see and know. The Bible says that they that are after the flesh mind the things of the flesh and after the Spirit the things of the Spirit.

The UnHindered Flow is a series of knowledge receptions revealed by the living Word of God. These receptions have come to us as gifts of God because we have humbly and fearfully made ourselves available to the Word of God in order to receive the full flow of spiritual knowledge. The Revelational Knowledge Institute is a systematic intentional cooperation of souls bound in faith and submission to Jesus Christ gathered with expectation of illumination from the Word of God. Wonderful illumination has been forthcoming as we have humbly made ourselves available by faith to the Word of God. We have a response of grateful praise and not celebration of our own capacity to obtain. We have received by grace and not by submitting the Word to our academic or scholastic aptitude. This series of receptions that has flowed unto us is identical with all revelation that is true.

Inasmuch as academics have approached God's Word without fear and without humility, we are academically disabled and we must approach in an old way, with fear and trembling and wait upon the Word to give us His revelation and receive from God's Word, an *unhindered flow* of revelation from God.

We consistently receive revelation from God's Word to be shared in these availability sessions for those who would submit under the Word of God for illumination reception. This may sound new, but we assure you that this is in keeping with historical Christianity and Old Testament doctrine. Nothing new, just clarifying the old. We are affiliated and in agreement with the tenants of the Tennessee and Southern Baptist Conventions.

Receptions

Out of the seals come the trumpets; out of the trumpets come the vials. It seems to be moving in sequential elements—moving from the general to the particular. It telescopes from the large to the focused.

In the same sense, God through Christ speaks first to the church, then to the one who would overcome—from the general to the focused individual. We see that process in Joshua as God brings Achan to justice. Amen.

INSTEAD OF THE FLOW, THE ACADEMIC WORLD RECEIVES TRICKLES

In the academic world, people study the Bible line upon line, precept upon precept, here a little, there a little.

Whom shall he teach knowledge? and whom shall he make to understand doctrine? them that are weaned

155

from the milk, and drawn from the breasts. For precept
must be upon precept, precept upon precept; line upon
line, line upon line; here a little, and there a little:
—Isa. 28: 9-10

This is the refreshing, yet they would not hear. But the Word of the Lord was upon them precept upon precept, here a little, there a little....

Does God really want to communicate with us line upon line, precept upon precept? *I don't think so.* He doesn't want people with stammering lips, wavering hearts, and no power to represent Him. But it has to be the demonstration of the Holy Ghost. They must be fearful and humble and still to receive the Word of God. Not glean it.... But the Word must impart unto us, flow unto us according to our fearful, humble submission unto it. Man does not want to come as a beggar, he wants to get it the hard way, and he wants to earn it.

THE PLOWMAN AND THE SOWER

Give ye ear, and hear my voice; hearken, and hear
my speech. Doth the plowman plow all day to sow?
doth he open and break the clods of his ground? When
he hath made plain the face thereof, doth he not cast
abroad the fitches, and scatter the cummin, and cast
in the principal wheat and the appointed barley and
the rie in their place? For his God doth instruct him to
discretion, and doth teach him. For the fitches are not
threshed with a threshing instrument, neither is a cart
wheel turned about upon the cummin; but the fitches

are beaten out with a staff, and the cummin with a rod. Bread corn is bruised; because he will not ever be threshing it, nor break it with the wheel of his cart, nor bruise it with his horsemen. This also cometh forth from the LORD of hosts, which is wonderful in counsel, and excellent in working.

—Isa. 28:23-29

The fruit comes by flailing and beating (threshing), beating it with the staff and rod. He talks of the Word, the seed and the ground.

God is the plowman and the sower. He plows up the ground and breaks up the clods. The plow cuts up the ground and then once the ground is broken up, he breaks the clods. If we are in big clods, we're too big to receive seed in our hearts and it won't be well received to do the work. The ground has to be made small.

When He's made plain the face thereof…the ground is even… then He waters and scatters the seed, each in its place, different kind of seed, each in its place.

The plowman…could possibly be Jesus Christ, or could possibly be a man working under the Lord. He is given discretion as to what to thresh and what to grind, and how to separate what is useful and what is not useful…using the staff and the rod.

This also cometh forth from the LORD of hosts, which is wonderful in counsel, and excellent in working

—Isa. 28:29

This scripture is talking about Babylon….

The Word of God is not going to benefit them because they are hearing and not receiving, because of their pride, their strong drink, as they sit at the table where they should be receiving meat. They had been weaned from milk, so they sit at the table, but the tables are filthy not clean. They cease to teach them knowledge; they will not be able to receive it because the way they receive it is like rote knowledge, like receiving empty training…academic vanity…therefore they could not receive it spiritually because they had no relationship with the one that was speaking. Foreigners had to teach it to them because they did not have enough sense to receive the word of rest. He tried to teach them about rest, but they had to learn precept upon precept. Their relationship did not help their communication because their relationship was dead, it was not spiritual.

Precepts and lines, just a little here and a little there so that they might fall backward and be broken. Hear the Word of the Lord, ye scornful men that rule this people which is in Jerusalem because you have said, we have made a covenant with death and with hell made an agreement.

We're not fighting death and hell. When the time of death and hell comes they believed it would not come to them. They had made a covenant with it and hid themselves under an illusion of eternal life.

Therefore thus saith the Lord GOD, Behold, I lay in Zion for a foundation a stone, a tried stone, a precious corner stone, a sure foundation: he that believeth shall not make haste.

—Isa. 28:16

The person that believes will not be on the run because of his sure foundation. Judgment is talking about being straight, nothing crooked, righteous will be measured straight, the refuge of lies, the hiding place for lies will be swept away. And the waters shall overflow the hiding place....

THE SPIRIT OF ADOPTION

The Word is capable of entering you. It is alive and powerful and is able to liberate you from your own stuff, from Satan's stuff, from everything that the world can cast upon you. It is able to make you walk at liberty as a child of God.

Do not receive the Word lightly, but let it enter you and let it reveal to you who you are. And if you are yet separated from God let the Word tell you something, that you might by decision be joined unto the Father because of your belief in the blood of the Son.

There is now no condemnation to them who are in Christ Jesus who walk not after the flesh but after the Spirit.

Walking after the Spirit is very well defined. Jesus said, "Thy Word is truth", and in reference to the Holy Ghost, He said, "He is the Spirit of truth," and Jesus Himself said, "I am the truth." God is called the Father of Spirits and the Father of the Truth. If you walk in the Spirit you will walk in the Word. It may be difficult sometimes that when we talk about the Spirit we are talking about the one who is the author of the Word of God. And the Holy Spirit is the teaching Spirit that brings us to the point where we are born of the Word.

Of His own will begot He us by the Word. Everybody who has been born again has been born by the reception of the Word of God because he believed it; he was a new creature, borne from above, by the Spirit by the Word. Everyone who is God's child had to be born again. Nobody becomes His child because they were nice, but by faith in the operation of God, which had to do with the dying of His Son on the cross, believing that that dying was a sacrifice, the sacrifice of the perfect Lamb made. There had to be a payment made that you could not make. Those who believed God when He said that the blood would take away the sin of the world and believed that they are included when God said whosoever will. *For God so loved the world that he gave his only begotten son and whosoever believeth on Him should not perish but have everlasting life.* As many as received him to them gave he the power to become the sons of God. There is therefore now no condemnation to them who are in Christ Jesus. Amen, amen. No condemnation.

It's not a good thing to go around making charges against the child of God unless you wish to confront him. For there is no condemnation to them who are in Christ Jesus. There is nothing you can accuse them of, nothing that you can say against them. If you know the things of their flesh, you can't accuse them of it; you can't hold it over them. There is *now,* not when you get to heaven, but right now! There is no condemnation to them who are in Christ Jesus who walk after the Spirit and not after the flesh.

Sin and death is the law of humanity. Death means to be totally separated from God. It's the second death.

Sin brings the second death. I want you to think of death and sin; absolute separation is the same thing as hell. The law of sin and death says I was born separated and if I do not reconcile with God I will stay separated. And if I die in that condition, that is absolute; there is nothing else I can do. If you enter into the separation of this body and you have not reconciled with God through the blood of the Lamb, there is no hope for you; there is nothing you can do, you are lost! You rejected Him until the last hour and you are forever separated from God. God is where light and peace comes from. You will know no light and no peace, only darkness and chaos, because you will never know anything that has anything to do with God. And the Bible lets us know that those who end up in that situation will seek relief and never find it. There is no goodness there because you cannot know anything that animates from the father. The flames of hell are talking about destruction and this destruction is never ending; you're always in process, you never get to the end, you are always in process without relief. Send Lazarus that he might but dip his finger in the water and put it on my tongue. Your torment will go on. The torment for a spiritual being is more than we can possibly imagine.

Condemned means that's where you're going and there is no way out. There is no condemnation for them who walk after the Spirit. Judging means condemning.

But if the Spirit of him that raised up Jesus dwells in you, he shall also quicken your mortal bodies; if you live after the flesh you shall die!

The sons of God are those whose steps are ordered by the Word of God. If not, you are not a son of God. The way is clear; it has been marked out and preached. You must hide the Word of God in your heart if you would not sin against Him. For you have not received the Spirit of bondage but you have received the Spirit of adoption.

That's what we're talking about, the Spirit of adoption! It has not come to pass yet in the material man, but it abides in us. It's a Spirit and He abides in us. Even though we still have bodies the Spirit of adoption is in us, hallelujah, but we have received the Spirit of adoption whereby we cry abba father. That's how the Jews say father, and *pater,* that's how the Gentiles have said father. I don't care if it's a Gentile or Jew, it's still a common father and he has come into our hearts and made us children and there is a cry made from the heart that calls on my father. Jesus said to the believers, pray unto Him. "Our Father." Nobody called God *Father* until Jesus got here. They called Him God, …but nobody called Him Father until Jesus said so. Because Jesus said go to Him in prayer and say, "Our Father!"

The Word that He spoke was life to them; it's always been life. When Jesus spoke, His Word was Spirit and those who received it had the Spirit of life abiding in them. They had the Spirit of God because the Word was in them. Even before He died they were even able to say Father, our Father. With us it's even more so. Because Christ died, because those who received Him were cleansed and those who were cleansed were also baptized into His death, they were buried and raised

His resurrection where they could say *Father*. They were Spirit being with the Spirit life abiding in them and therefore had every right to say, "Our Father." You can call on Him. Some folks want to say God of Abraham, Isaac and Jacob, Oh Wonderful Creator. Jesus said say, "Our Father!" He has sent the Spirit into us, the Spirit that cries out, "Our Father." I know you can't believe it or hear it, but Jesus said it. So the Word of God cries out, "Abba, Father!" Listen everyone! In this life, when you are in trouble, you need to call to the Father! Call on Him! Every day call on Him!

> *The Spirit itself beareth witness with our spirit, that we are the children of God.*
> —Rom. 8:16

You know there are things that the saints do that those in the flesh just can't bring themselves to do. You need to get with the saints and you need to operate with the saints.

No matter how much agreement there is in the world. What's true, what's right? If we follow the Spirit of truth, then we are the children of God

The creature; there is a part of you that is a creature. Even if you are born again you have flesh. The Spirit is uncreated. It is God; the Spirit that resides in you is the Father. It's the divinity that comes to you from God to His children. There's a part of you that's creature.

> *For the earnest expectation of the creature waiteth for the manifestation of the sons of God.*
> —Rom. 8:19

That means so it can be seen. My physical being is waiting …the creature…my physical being is waiting for that thing that happens, for when my physical being becomes actually the son of God… my flesh…. for the creature was made subject to vanity… your flesh was made subject to nothingness.

The created part is yearning even though it is subject to death, it still yearns for adoption because it is going to get delivered from death.

He has subjected my flesh that my flesh would dare to hope.

Did you know there is something about you in the flesh that shall get up out of corruption…. rotting…deterioration…there is something about you that shall never rot…that is incorruptible even thou it is flesh… if you are a child of God then your physical self is waiting for that day.

Because the creature itself will be delivered from that bondage.

For we know that the whole creation groaneth and travaileth in pain together until now.

Even we ourselves groan within ourselves… we are blessed; we have the promise that we are the children of God, but we're not satisfied yet. That groaning is our yearning. We yearn for something more…but there is something else and what we are and have is not enough.

Even we ourselves groan within ourselves waiting for the adoption to wit….

To wit means know this…. This is what you need to know…what are they groaning for….

To wit...the redemption of our body. The redemption of the body hasn't happened yet for anyone other than Jesus. His body was resurrection...the redemption of His body.

For we are saved by hope.

The Spirit helpeth our infirmities...He prays because we yet have to be changed into the image of Jesus Christ. It sometimes takes pain to change; it takes sorrow to change and we are not able to go to God and say give me some pain.

Only He knows what to ask for...only He knows.... I cannot ask for what I need. I don't know what I need to be changed into His image. What I need may be something painful or sorrowful and I in myself am too protective of self to ask for that! The Spirit prays for me!

I can't get depressed, distraught, because all things are working together to mold me into the image of Jesus Christ. I can rest assured that God is in the process and He's doing something for me. I can say, "Lord I trust you." And He that searched the heart knoweth!

HALLELUJAH! HALLELUJAH! HALLELUJAH!

SALVATION OF THE SOUL

When the flesh is born, it is a soul. We speak this as defined in New Testament terms, the human life. The soul can experience a death, but not annihilation. The soul is the life given by God and every man has this special soul. The soul can experience a destruction that has no end, but will forever be in process. The salvation that we are seeking as souls is that we should never know that never-ending process of soul destruction which we call hell. Only by a birth of life that is from God and the transference of our soul to Christ in the resurrection and ascension—only by this can we be saved from soul destruction. Our soul is then hid in Christ. Our life (soul) hid in Christ and the soul (life) that we have which we call Spirit, that born again non-material birth that is by the Word of God through faith by the divine operation of the Father is our means of having the life of Christ abide in us (Galatians 2:20; Romans 6:3; Ephesians 2:6; Ephesians 3:16).

The saving of our lives equals the saving of our souls and our lives are hid with God in Christ Jesus. John the first chapter tells us that the Word gave us light. He lighted every man that cometh into the world. That means that our lives were granted to us from the Christ Himself when we came into the world.

This is the life of the flesh. Now He comes to those to whom He has granted life in the flesh, that they might be Spirit born by faith in the Word, but they refused to recognize Him as the life-giver. But as many as received Him (the Word), to them gave He power to become the sons of God. This, however, could not transpire until He was crucified and resurrected and all of those who are crucified with Him have a soul deposit in Him and now live by His divine life in that He has exchanged life with them. We understand then how the soul is saved. It is saved in Christ Jesus. It is saved because sin no longer has dominion over the life in that it has died already and paid the penalty of death. And having died is hid in Christ. That is safety. *We are saved!*

Crucified with Christ, seated at the right hand of the Father in Christ Jesus!

For ye are dead, and your life is hid with Christ in God.

—Col. 3:3

When Christ, who is our life, shall appear, then shall ye also appear with him in glory.

—Col. 3:4

THE SPIRITUAL VESSEL AND THE CARNAL VESSEL

We must not subject the Word to our carnal gray matter for that is flesh, but the Word is spiritually discerned and it is spiritually revealed. Hallelujah!

The human mind asks why! When things don't make sense the human mind asks why, as in the battle of Jericho and Naaman dipping seven times in the Jordan. Nicodemus, after being told by Jesus that he must be born again to see and enter into the kingdom, asked how can these things be?

They are spiritually discerned and if we look at them with our fleshly eye and try to understand them with our fleshly minds, we come to non sequitur and surely we come to conflict. There are many things written in the Word that our carnal minds cannot approach in cleanness and we must seek to package them in our understanding. There is much in the Word that is too big to fit into our understanding if we recognize our understanding to be that which we process in our brains but they are spiritually received and spiritually revealed.

What I mean by approaching in cleanness is the vessel that would hold the knowledge—it shapes it, colors it, and otherwise modifies it.

If the vessel that holds it be my carnal mind, then it will be shaped and colored by carnality and capacity limitations. If the vessel that holds it be spiritual then the content will be neither shaped nor colored, neither hindered nor corrupted, for the spiritual mind is motivated by the Spirit and answered in the spirit by the Spirit. This is perfect communication: like for like; kind for kind.

We have two vessels. The new creature is comprised of the "old man" which is carnal, and the "new man" which is born of God from above by faith in Christ Jesus. The new man is called the spirit man and the old man is called the carnal. Spiritual content is for the Spirit-man. The carnal mind cannot receive spiritual things but the nature of the carnal mind is proud and self-seeking, self-projecting. The Holy Spirit directs us for spiritual content and the carnal mind motivates us for carnal content. The Spirit will not need to subject Himself to scrutiny by foreign and finite mindset. The Holy Spirit knows the things of the Spirit and is able to edify the spirit man.

For they that are after the flesh do mind the things of the flesh; but they that are after the Spirit the things of the Spirit.

—Rom. 8:5

For to be carnally minded is death; but to be spiritually minded is life and peace.

—Rom. 8:6

Because the carnal mind is enmity against God: for it is not subject to the law of God, neither indeed can be.

—Rom. 8:7

So then they that are in the flesh cannot please God.

—Rom. 8:8

But ye are not in the flesh, but in the Spirit, if so be that the Spirit of God dwell in you. Now if any man have not the Spirit of Christ, he is none of his.

—Rom. 8:9

If we would receive spiritual things we must understand it as reception and not as seizing. The Holy Spirit desires to reveal but as it has been said elsewhere in this writing He resisteth the proud and gives grace to the humble. Again we must recognize humility is proper before the almighty Word of God.

If I approach the Word with curiosity, I am restricted. If I approach it by necessity, whatever I deem my necessity to be shall color or shape the content that I will receive. If some dissatisfaction should cause me to approach the Word then the seeking of satisfaction will restrict or expand the content in relationship to the expectation of my carnal striving.

That which is of me that is Spirit resides in my carnal being. But I believe that my carnal being resides in my spirit man.

And I believe that at the direction of the Holy Spirit, my spirit being is able to bring to my mouth those things to bring to others. And by their faith they become born and by their birth they are able to receive revelation.

All that God has revealed in me that is spiritual I believe resides in my spirit man. I believe that it speaks to my brain and to my mouth that which I should share in my spirit man.

I do not believe my carnal being holds spiritual knowledge. It does not have the wherewithal to process it. I believe that the Word of God is alive and it manipulates my brain and my mouth with those things that I have been open to receive in my spirit man. I believe that is the way it is with all of us who are born spirit. Everything in the Word teaches me that.

When you begin to believe God, there is a birth that takes place within you; it is like a seed that is planted. And by the reception of God's Word you grow up into a spirit being. You mature and grow up as you add to your belief in that Word and become capable of reproduction…By faith…by the hearing of the Word we have faith but it's a strange thing that faith comes by hearing because hearing comes by the Word. That means I cannot have faith to hear unless I've got the Word abiding in me. So I can't hear unless I get the Word of God, and it is believing or having faith in what I hear that brings me to faith… and faith is where birth comes from!

The thing has to have something living in the process beyond what I have in the flesh because in my flesh dwelleth no good thing. And my flesh cannot hear or receive spiritual things. So what is it that causes me by the hearing of the Word to come to faith? It has something to do with the fact that the Word has its own mind. It has its own capacity to generate and to give birth. It is alive… it is quickening. It's not by him that *runneth or wills* but it is of God that we are born and it is beyond figuring out. When we seek Him with our whole heart, he has already done some birthing in us by the Word.

It's a paradox beyond comprehension.

SPIRITUAL GIFTS

You cannot have the Word of wisdom without the Word of knowledge, so if I speak a Word of wisdom it is spoken out of the content which we call knowledge. The Word of wisdom and Word of knowledge are given together and not separated at all.

Knowledge comes from revelation; wisdom comes from the presence of the Holy Spirit. Wisdom is the capacity to use knowledge. Prophets must have the gift of wisdom and gift of knowledge; receiving from the Word of God is revelation. Understanding what God is saying is knowledge. What is He is saying, what is He communicating? God's communication spoken through a human is a prophet, that's what makes him a prophet. To speak God's communication cannot be done unless you have in your spirit revelation of God's Word, and prophecy is itself wisdom from God. Do you represent Him, do you love Him, is it truth from the Lord? Is it the Word of God and is it being communicated by that person? Knowledge, wisdom, understanding in the Bible—God is the only one who can decipher which is which and where it's divided.

Receive this. Receive it wholly holy (fully sanctified). Do not try to break it down with your brain. You don't need to be able to break it down; don't treat the Word with your brain, but allow the Word to treat your brain. I can't break this for you, you receive this with your spirit. Let your brain stay out of it and God as you need will show you how to use it, how to know it.

It will be in your spirit. When He gets ready He can make you brilliant! He can make you so brilliant that all the doctors in theology will just have to hush. Then at times He can make you just sit still and quiet.

Communicating God's Word under the behest of the Holy Spirit is prophesying.

GOD ALLOWS US TO WALK OUT WHAT'S IN OUR HEARTS

According to Jeremiah 17:9-10, "*The heart is deceitful and above all things desperately wicked. Who can know it?*" The Lord searches the heart. We have things in our hearts that we ourselves are not aware of. We have deceived ourselves into thinking that our hearts are clean and pure. There are things that we would do if we were placed in certain situations that would surprise us! God steps back and lets us walk out what is in our heart so that we can repent and He can cleanse us.

MIND OVER MATTER

Mind over matter. Spiritual over physical. Even to be able to think is spiritual. The thought need not necessarily have God as its source, but the realm is spiritual and there is much attempted input into our minds. How can we not believe in a Spiritual realm in the light of the normal spiritual reality that we are living in?

RE: SEPT 11, 2001, TWIN TOWERS DISASTER

This is a milestone, a message back to humanity along with the many messages that have said that man left alone is incapable of self-governance. Inasmuch as he was a free being, God allowed him to make the decision for self-governance. The ramifications of the knowledge (fruit) are still working itself out by God's permissive will. Man is seeing the effects of self-governance without God. Sometimes the question is asked, "Why has God allowed this evil to come upon us?" It is God's intent to do a minimum of interference while the knowledge fruit shows man who he is. Sin in the world—not simply personal sin, not just national sin—but sin in the world finds out all of mankind, the righteous and the unrighteous. We are all subject to the effects of sin and death that reverberate out of our separation from our Creator. God is not evil in that He allows man this age wherein man rules himself, but by His longsuffering God allows each man to come to the knowledge of his need to be reconciled with Him. Many men however, will always refuse to recognize his inability to righteously govern himself. The towers at both ends of history have the job of indicating man's love for himself, pride in himself, even in the midst of failure.

Man's self-dependence is man's desire to depend upon himself instead of God, to know his reality, and to carry out good. But only in the Word of God is there a consistency between what is written and what I see in myself and what I see in the world.

At one time man considered that when he knew God, this was the age of innocence, but this was more the age of wisdom. Because man was created with the inborn capacity to fear God and thereby have wisdom in that man sought God for all things. When man became a fool by knowledge having eaten of the tree, then man became innocent or better ignorant in his knowledge calling himself wise. He became a fool for the first time in his existence; man in his own eyes became naked.

Tower of Babel

There is immediate good in seeking to punish the wicked who have behaved murderously, but over time the good shall swing according to Scripture and become the true evil in that it denies the sovereignty of God.

Man will have the ambition that it had before as it resurrects these towers. The concept that includes all gods is not a good concept because this pervasive acceptance of equal sovereignty amongst the gods allows sovereignty to none of them, therefore renders none of them in human estimation to be god. Inclusion of all gods is to deny any god. For the attributes of God is that he "alone" is sovereign with all power and all wisdom.

He alone is God with none else beside Him. The God of the Christians and the Jews is one God and He is a jealous God; that is His name. If there is not that one, then there is no god; hence, atheism. The concept of all gods is equal to no god. The tower in the beginning was the rallying point for a unified humanity sans God. The resurrection of the twin towers shall also be the rallying point for new human unity. Here man will change into the new world order. Wherein evil is that which is an affront to human dignity, and good is that which is of the consensus. For the consensus shall be equal to the New Testament in its use as a directive by humanity. That which does the most good for the most people shall be considered the highest good and any who are not called to the purpose of the highest good shall be hated and an offense to humanity. This shall be the basis of the government of anti-Christ after many events and changes. The government shall be upon his shoulders.

To order additional copies of

How to know
THE UNHINDERED
FLOW
OF GOD'S REVELATION

Have your credit card ready and call:

1-877-421-READ (7323)

or please visit our web site at
www.pleasantword.com

Also available at:
www.amazon.com
and
www.barnesandnoble.com

Printed in the United States
47857LVS00001B/109-282

9 781414 104386